CW00344335

Dai and Let Live

DAI JONES

gomer

First Impression – 2004
Second Impression – 2004
Third Impression – 2004

ISBN 1 84323 457 2

Fi Dai sy' 'ma by Dai Jones
was originally published by Gwasg Gwynedd in 1997.

Printed in Wales at
Gomer Press, Llandysul, Ceredigion

To my
granddaughter,
Celine

My thanks go to the people of Wales for the honour of entertaining them for over 30 years; to my friends in the media for their loyalty and friendship; to my family for always being there and to my neighbours for making home such a special place. I'm also grateful to Lyn Ebenezer for squeezing my life into the pages of this book so that you can enjoy the most important thing of all – a laugh!

Diolch i bawb.
Dai Jones
Llanilar

1

The Little Londoner

I was born at the Royal Hospital, Hornsey, London on the eighteenth of October, 1943. It seems that I arrived soon after dinner. Mam timed it well. She loved her food.

People imagine me to be a dyed-in-the-wool Cardi. But a substantial part of my being is Cockney. My roots, it's true, lie deep in the earth of Ceredigion. But I was three years old when I moved to Wales.

My father was a Cardi. My mother was a Cardi. She hailed from Talybont while my father was from Llangwrddon. Or, to be exact, from Lledrod, which is but a few miles further west. Dad was one of ten children, and Mam one of three. Like many Cardis before them, they emigrated to London, the land of milk and money. Or so they had visualized it. And it was there that they both met.

Dad found a job with Dickie Davies, Caledonian Road. And this is where one of the many coincidences that have shaped my life occurred. Dickie Davies was Dad's first employer in London, and his son, Ieuan, was the producer of *Siôn a Siân,* the Welsh version of *Mr and Mrs,* when I started presenting the show on HTV.

Mam's parents, John and Jane Jones, Grandad and Grandma Talybont, whom we knew as Tad-cu and Mam-gu, had long moved to London before my father arrived there. Work was scarce in the Ceredigion heartland, and off they went to the English capital. And there they kept alive a little bit of the old county – its customs and, especially, its chapel-going tradition. They seldom missed a service at Castle Street chapel where the Revd Walter P. John, formerly of Pontarddulais, was the minister.

Strangely, when Tad-cu and Mam-gu travelled on the London buses and conversed in Welsh, people would mistake them for Italians. As well as speaking a strange language, they were small in stature. Mam was small. And despite the fact that Dad's family were all tall, he was the exception. And both my parents were on the stocky side. It is therefore no surprise that I am also well-blessed paunch-wise.

Tad-cu worked first of all at United Dairies in Willesden. But such was his *hiraeth,* his deep longing for the land, that he decided to work with the horses. Thus he could bridge the geographical as well as the social chasm between London and Ceredigion. At that time some eighty horses would be out on the rounds. And it was there, with the horses, that he spent the rest of his working life.

Dad was one of two of the ten children to head for London in his search for work. He loved the *hwyl,* the love of life, and he was prepared to take a gamble. During the holidays, at Easter especially, many of those who had left for London and had set up their own businesses, would return to their old localities and visit their families. There, on land where they had once scraped a living, they would encounter strapping lads tilling and toiling. Feeling that they could do with some extra help, they would approach some of them to offer them work. It usually happened after the Sunday night chapel service. They knew that these country lads had work in their sinews. And one Sunday night, following the service at Tabor chapel, Dickie Davies,

8

having been impressed by my father's work, coaxed him to leave the land and join him in London.

Dad had set his sights on being a minister. Country lads had a choice of two ambitions in those days, the cloth or the school. Ministers and teachers were revered. Dad was very friendly with Trefor Lloyd, Ty'r Helyg, who did become a minister – thus achieving what Dad never did. Both of them had attended school at Lledrod and they shared the same interests. Dad, apparently, when he was a lad, would meticulously chronicle the minister's sermon in a notebook that he always took with him to chapel.

But London enticed him, and off he went. He first spent his time doing the milk rounds after first filling the bottles. And it was there that he met Mam. It was also where we, all three of us children, were born.

Then, when I was about three years old, my brother Trefor and I spent a holiday with my uncle and aunt who farmed Ty'n Cefen back in Llangwrddon. Uncle Morgan and Aunty Hannah gave us all the love that they would have bestowed on their own children, had they been blessed with any.

Trefor, incidentally, who is younger than I by two years, still lives in London where he runs a taxi service. And I well remember, just before I first flew from Heathrow, Trefor phoning me to tell me to look out for him.

'When you arrive at the airport, look out for a red taxi', he said. 'That will be mine.'

Now, I was quite used to seeing black taxis. In fact I had been led to believe that all taxis were black. I had never seen a red cab. But when I reached Heathrow, there, weaving their way in all directions like hyperactive ants were hundreds of red taxis. I never saw Trefor. But, my God, I saw some red taxis.

Anyway, I arrived a bewildered little Cockney in Llangwrddon, in the heart of the countryside. And quite simply, as soon as I arrived I had no wish to return to London. When I made this known to Uncle and Aunty, they were delighted. And they assured me that if I wanted to stay, then both Trefor and I were welcome to do so. And since my parents were busy – they had started up their own business by then – Morgan and Hannah encouraged us to stay. And stay we did.

I would, naturally, go back to London occasionally to visit my parents. When I was there I would long for the country. Yet, by the time I reached my early teens, I would look forward to my London visits when I would spend my time in my parents' shop and on the milk-round. But after a few weeks I would once again yearn for the smell of the countryside – the scent of new-mown hay, even the smell of cow dung. And it wouldn't be long before I was back there.

I still retain some fond memories of London. I remember, for instance, a certain Mrs. Challis. This Mrs. Challis had fifteen children. She would occasionally help Dad in the shop. And in lieu of payment she would be given free groceries to feed herself and her numerous offspring. That would be her wage. And I well remember Dad helping her carry her overloaded shopping bags home every Friday night.

One particular sight will remain in my memory for ever. It was the night that the War ended. There, on top of our local air-raid shelter, stood all fifteen of Mrs Challis's brood, raucously singing *God Save the King.* But rather than join in their celebrations, the rather unpatriotic matriarch bellowed, 'Bugger the King. Get inside and wash yourselves.'

Much of the social life of the district revolved around the shop. I can still remember the official address: R.I. Jones &

Sons, 17 Kingsdown Road, Hornsey, London, N19. The shop would be open from seven in the morning till seven in the evening. On Sunday it would close around dinner-time. My parents would then attend St Padarn's Church. It was only later, that they began attending Mam's chapel in Castle Street.

The order of the service in London differed from that which I was used to in Llangwrddon. During the sermon in London, all of us kids would troop downstairs. We were spared the minister's discourse. At such times the other children would beg me to tell them stories about life in the country back in Wales. I remember explaining to them, amongst other things, that we kept cattle in Ceredigion, and that as part of my duties I would have to clean the dung from under the cows. The word for that kind of work in Welsh is *carthu*. And when one of the children asked me the meaning of that word I told him that *carthu* meant just that, simply clearing dung. The lady teacher rebuked me for being so crude. But it was great fun. There we were, thirty or more of us children – and I was quietly pleased that I was the only one who knew what clearing dung really meant.

We all conversed in Welsh. All, that is, apart from Gwyn Laing, who was from anglicized Neath. It was the norm to see a hundred or more attending the services at Castle Street. And ever-present, always sitting on the gallery behind the clock, would be Tad-cu and Mam-gu. Immediately behind them would sit Dr Terry James, who would later make his name as a musician in Hollywood. He was in sole charge of the Castle Street choir. Tad-cu was a member of that choir. He was an accomplished tenor who had been taught by Sir Walford Davies back in Aberystwyth.

But it was in the country that I felt most at ease. And I believe that the reason for this was to do more with time than with anything else. Back in Llangwrddon there was time for everything. London was one big mad rush, so much so that returning to Wales to the unfettered freedom, to the pure fresh air, and especially to the animals, was pure heaven. There, life moved at a measured, more leisurely pace. And yet, when school holidays came around and I returned to London, I was able to enjoy the best of both worlds.

And they were two separate, two completely different worlds. In Llangwrddon, following the Sunday service, no-one would even contemplate a pint of beer. But in London, following the evening meeting, Mam would take us children to Lyons Corner House for Sunday supper. The men, on the other hand, would aim for the Holyrood in the West End for a beer. In London, the chapel and the pub would go hand in hand – the synagogue and the tavern, as that great Welsh poet, R. Wiliams Parry, so aptly wrote.

One memory that I still treasure is that of delivering milk around the various factories on my bike. I would have been about 15 years old, riding a bike which boasted a big, square carrier jutting from under the handlebars. Just like a butcher's bike. And as I would alight it would tend to dip its nose because of all the weight above the front wheel. I broke many a milk bottle as a result of that.

Another memory that remains fresh in my mind is that of the goods stored in every nook and cranny of the shop and the house. When I would visit during the school holidays my bedroom would be chock-a-block with all sorts of boxes. And when, because of the noise of the traffic, I couldn't sleep, I would read whatever was written on the

12

boxes. And I firmly believe that it was from reading *Quaker Oats* and *Corn Flakes* boxes that I learnt English. There were boxes everywhere. And without a word of a lie, the first thing I would see on exiting the toilet would be a cardboard box proclaiming that *Wilson's Makes Your Dog Happy.*

My friends back in Llangwrddon knew very little English. I remember Islwyn Brynchwith, my cousin, coming up to London to spend his school holiday with me. One afternoon Mam demanded that we should all have our photograph taken together. There we were, the four of us in a photographic studio – myself, my brother Trefor, my sister Glenys, and Islwyn – Mam had gone to the toilet. And along came the photographer.

'All right then kids,' he said. 'Do you want your photo taken together as a group? All four of you?'

He spoke with a perfect Cockney accent. After a full half-minute's silence, his face blushing like a rose, Islwyn answered.

'Yes, we want to pull the photos together.' And pointing to us all in turn, he added. 'You can pull us all, me, him, she and it.'

The shop was a virtual treasure store. Dad sold almost everything – cheese, bacon, goods of all sorts. And milk, of course. Once, returning with my father to re-open the shop after the dinner break, I well recall seeing three suspicious-looking characters lurking outside. By this time Dad had opened his second shop in Lancia Road. I was not to know it at the time, but the three men were there for one specific reason – to rob the till. My father quickly read the situation and, in Welsh, he told me to run like hell to tell the local bobby who lived up the street to come down immediately.

13

This I did. The policeman lifted me on his shoulders and galloped to the shop where he arrested all three. That was the first time I ever saw a Black Maria as the three unsuccessful thieves were driven away.

That incident underlines the usefulness of speaking Welsh. If Dad had urged me in English to fetch the policeman then the men would have understood him and would surely have stopped me.

My parents managed to settle well in London. Dad liked his pint and was quite a dab hand at bowls. Indeed, at the Aberville Bowling Club in Turnpike Lane he was a champion. He also loved watching soccer and became an avid Arsenal fan. He would often go to see them at Highbury while we, the children, played around Finsbury Park.

When they chose to leave the trade, the two decided to move and spend their hard-earned retirement at Horsham in Sussex. The business had been put on the market and they had arranged for friends to run the shops until they were sold. But cruelly, on the very morning when they should have moved, my father suffered a stroke. He was paralysed down one side of his body. And that's how he remained until he died eight years later.

Following Dad's death Mam remained in Horsham. Glenys, the youngest of us children, who is married, also lived nearby. Mam died three years ago after a short illness. At 88 years old she dressed herself for the hospital visit and that was the first time for her to be hospitalized since my birth over 60 years previously. She had made plans for all the mourners, after the funeral, to congregate at the local pub for tea and free drinks till 8.30 in the evening. That was Mam all over.

The language of the home was always Welsh in London.

14

And often in the shop, when they didn't want any outsiders to know their business, my parents would deliberately converse in the language of Heaven. Yet, even though I was brought up to be Welsh through and through, I am proud of the fact that I was born a Cockney. Whenever I work with a new film crew I will often tease them by addressing them in English with a real Cockney accent. And John, my son, is quite as adept as I am.

I admire the Cockney. He's a real character. I love watching those old Alf Garnett programmes and *Only Fools and Horses.* Alf and Del Boy are brilliantly authentic characters.

I remember, while traipsing around the streets holding on to my mother's hand, some of the locals addressing Mam. ''Allo there, Peggy Dick. 'Ow are ya?' Because my father's name was Dick she, naturally, became Peggy Dick. They took it for granted that Dad owned Mam.

Both my parents spoke English with a natural Cockney accent. I remember going to London to record some programme or other at the Alexandra Palace and Dad ordering a taxi on my behalf. 'I want to order a taxi for a Mr David Jones. 'E's goin' to Ally Pally,' he said. I had no idea where he was sending me. It could have been somewhere in India as far as I knew. And when the taxi arrived I was sure that India was my destination. The driver was an Asian gentleman who wore a turban. And anxious to please him I explained, in my best English, 'I'd like to go to the Alexandra Palace, please.' He answered me in pure Cockney. 'I know, mate, Ally Pally.'

Anyone hearing Mam speaking English would swear she was an East-ender born and bred. And my sister Glenys is exactly the same. Mam, by the way – and many of those

15

who have met her have said this – looked the spitting image of Maggie Post, a character from the Welsh television soap opera *Pobol y Cwm*. She was exactly the same size and shape – and was just as talkative as Maggie.

Mam once had to ring Dad's employer to inform him that her husband was indisposed and couldn't go to work that day. In her most respectable English accent she said, 'I'm very sorry, but my husband isn't able to come to work today. He's suffering with diarrhoea.' Back came the answer from the boss, 'Aw, bloody 'ell, Mrs Jones, I can't spell that. I'll put "the shits" dahn instead.'

Yes, Cockneys. A rare breed. There's no-one to compare with them.

Even though my heart was in the country I would, despite the fact that I only spent short visits in London, miss some of my friends in the city. The Cockney, to me, is very much like the Cardi. He's a great character and is basically kind and welcoming. To me, the Cockney isn't English. I often feel that the Cockney is really a Celt. There is nothing arrogant or pompous about him. And he's always ready to share whatever he has.

To both Cockney and Cardi, humour plays an important role. Both can take the heat out of an altercation by cracking a joke. This is also true of the Irish, and they were there as well in large numbers. They had their own church, a small tin building not far from the shop. They all attended on Sunday mornings and they were so numerous that no less than three services had to be organized for them. Dad welcomed the custom of the Irish. They loved the white, fatty bacon that others would refuse. They would buy it by the bagful.

My parents, I suppose, represented the beginning of the

end of the golden age that the London Welsh enjoyed. They were two of many who had settled there and had become a part of the Welsh way of life in the city. In some ways their life became a microcosm of the one they had left behind. The London Welsh club at Grays Inn Road flourished, and there were numerous societies. And London at that time had much to offer the Welsh exiles. Welsh Nonconformity for them became more relaxed and less stringent in its unwritten rules. Dad would pop in to the local pub every dinner hour. And every evening, after the shop closed, he would play bowls.

And there was no shortage of friends from the old county who had settled in the area. I would often call to see Tom and Leis Lloyd at The Candy Bar in 555 Holloway Road. Leis – her name is a Welsh diminutive of Elizabeth – was from Llangwrddon, Dad's home village. I have always known her as Leis Cornel. The name Cornel, incidentally, is the Welsh name for Corner, the name of Leis's former home. And I have retained the connection with Tom and Leis over the years. Whenever I visited London for a singing engagement I would call to see them.

Another from the old locality was Steve Davies from Llangeitho who, like many other Cardi exiles, had a milk round. And an uncle, one of Dad's brothers, Uncle Wil, lived in Priory Road, Muswell Hill. The Cardis were there in strength. And like other exiles, whether Irish or Italians, they would stick together.

Despite the loosening of the old Nonconformist fetters, Dad would adhere religiously to custom. He would get up at four o'clock every morning. Then, at dinner-time, he would close for an hour. This routine was almost carved in stone. And during that hour, while drinking a pint or eating his meal, he would never take off his apron. And after his meal

17

he would take a break during which he dozed, the daily newspaper covering his face, until it was time to re-open the shop again. The newspaper, I suppose, helped close his mind from the rest of the world. Or did it help his thoughts to take flight far from the London smoke back to the hills and clear air of Ceredigion? I have often wondered about it. I would like to think that I'm right.

I have watched television programmes which have tried to recreate the old days in London. But mostly, I have found them to be fanciful and artificial. They do not portray the close-knit community that would meet regularly, especially on Saturday nights, to help keep alive their Welsh tongue and replenish their memories. There was a great sense of community, of affinity. I would often see Dad, having run out of this or that in the shop, ringing one of his friends in the trade. Wil Caledonian, perhaps. 'Wil, I've run out of butter. Can you help?' And Wil, if he had any in stock, would immediately dispatch whatever he could spare at the time. That's what it was all about.

To someone from the country, used to rural ways, it must have presented a strange picture. But to others, especially those who had come from the industrial south, it would seem fairly normal. In the Rhondda, as in London, buses ran regularly all day. In a place like Llangwrddon you might see one bus a week.

But if anything bridged the distance and made exiles feel at home in London it was this feeling of community, of good neighbourliness. The Cardis themselves were well-thought of in London. The bank would always be ready to lend them money. The bankers knew that the Cardi was willing to work. I'm afraid that the Englishman, basically, is not like that. Or at least he wasn't then. The Cardi – like the

Welsh in general – is a willing worker. While the Cockney enjoyed a good time, drinking into the early hours, the Cardi would be hard at work all hours of the day. And most of the night. There would only be time to relax on Saturday night and Sunday.

Though born in London, I would not consider myself to be a London Welshman. I would rather be known as a London Cardi – and I am proud to be one, even though we are reputed to be rather parsimonious. I have heard of a cattle-food salesman whose round covered the old county of Dyfed. In Pembrokeshire, if he was given a cup of tea with no sugar, the farmer's wife would say, 'I'm sorry. Take the sugar bowl.' In Carmarthenshire he would be told, 'There's no sugar in your tea. But take a spoonful.' But in Cardiganshire, if he found that there was no sugar in the tea he would be told, 'Are you sure you've stirred it?'

My parents spent the war years in London. And it was at that time that Dad worked as an auxiliary fireman in King's Cross. One night he was called out to a fire caused by enemy bombs. He helped carry out a mother and son. But they were already dead. He and the other men, however, did manage to save the father and daughter. It was only later that he realized that the two he had saved were from Llanfarian, just a few miles from his old home in Cardiganshire. The daughter, Gillian, later returned to Llanfarian to keep a pub, The Royal Oak, with her husband, Ken Joel. They retired some years ago and Ken later died. Yes, another of those strange coincidences.

Following the war, my parents bought what had been a shoe shop in an area which had been bombed flat. And soon they were employing eight staff who went out every day with trolleys and vans. That's how it all started for them.

19

Next door lived Bill and Elsie Thomas from Neath. They and their son, David, kept a sweet shop. These were the only two shops left in the area. That meant business was good. And almost overnight, my father was transformed from being a servant to a substantial employer.

Today, the place has changed completely: and looking at it now I feel glad that I was raised in the country. My decision to stay in Wales was not a conscious one. It wasn't sentiment and it certainly had nothing to do with love of the Welsh way of life or anything like that. For one thing, I was far too young to even think of such things. No, the attraction to me was something far more selfish – being given the chance to drive a tractor, for instance, being asked to choose a pup from among a litter. With that kind of freedom, who would want to return to live in London?

And Uncle Morgan was well aware of that. He would bring me into discussions. 'Do you want to look after this little calf? Or should I sell it?' My answer would be immediate. 'Oh, I'd like to keep him, Uncle Moc.' Yes, it was blackmail. But it was harmless blackmail. And because he and Aunty Hannah were childless, I helped fill a void in their lives. My presence there meant a lot to them.

Yes, my acceptance of country life was as natural to me as that offered to an old mountain sheep. Wherever it finds greener grass it tends to linger there. Just you leave a gate open for a sheep and it will go to wherever suits it best. And that's exactly what I did.

After all those years, the wheel has turned a full circle. And once more that old coincidence has struck. My father was first employed as a young farmhand at Argoed, Llangwrddon. Today I rent that very farm.

2

A Little Learning

Formal education, both mine and Trefor's, began at the local primary school at Llangwrddon. I well remember the headmistress, Mrs M.M. Andrews dispatching two of the pupils, Dai Ty'n Llwyn and Glenys Penbont to escort me there on my first day. Glenys, incidentally, was later to marry the broadcaster and presenter, Sulwyn Thomas. He didn't improve her though! She was Glenys Thomas back then in her school days. And she's still Glenys Thomas.

I was made welcome from the very beginning by the other kids. And I immediately warmed to them. I just wanted to do whatever they did.

We had two teachers at Llangwrddon school. One was Megan Williams. Outside the school, everyone knew her as Megan Maenelin. She later married the Revd Neville Morris, who became a minister at Carno. She was a very kind woman. Our headmistress, as I have already mentioned, was Mrs Andrews.

Naturally, our playtime diversions were no different from those of any normal pupils in any rural school. The girls would play house while the boys played tag. But I had a local hero, D.C. Morgan the butcher, who had his own slaughterhouse. He was also a local councillor. So whatever games the others played, I would be a butcher. Considering my love for meat, this was not unexpected.

I would set out my shop on the wall below the school. The cuts of meat would be stones collected from the nearby field, stones of various sizes. One day, among my customers was Ann Cornel. She wanted meat for threshing day, an important annual occasion for farmers. I realized that I didn't have a stone large enough in the shop for such a large gathering. So out I went over the wall to Cae Felin to fetch a huge stone for Ann. The daft things we used to do as kids!

I would also run around the yard pretending I was driving the meat van on my rounds. I would create such strange engine noises that my jaws would ache for the rest of the day. Brrrm! Brrrm! Brrrm!

Occasionally some of the other pupils would play shop. But since we were taught by two women, there was very little physical training. There were no formal games either. We never saw a proper football. The only ball kicked or thrown around was a small rubber ball. And that would somehow always land on the road below. We gouged deep brown tracks in the grass from running down to retrieve the ball.

It was only when a student trainee, Wil Griffiths, came to teach us that we played soccer for the very first time. He even formed a team. Later he was appointed headmaster at Commins Coch school near Aberystwyth. As a college student he was well acquainted with the game and he created quite a stir during his short stay.

Another important member of staff was the school cook, who also doubled as the cleaner. She was Mrs James, Rhos y Garreg. She was from the Rhondda and possessed a rich contralto voice. I well remember her singing in the school's Christmas concert.

In those days the food would be prepared on the school

premises. Nowadays the fashion is for the food to be prepared in advance centrally, and then ferried to the various rural schools. Mrs James had one particular favourite among the pupils. He was Dai Ty'n Llwyn. We all realized this and accepted it. Dai would sit next to me at the head of the table. And sometimes I would try to slide into Dai's place. I would do this especially when something I really fancied was on the menu – a fruit tart, for instance. By sliding slyly into Dai's place I would expect a large portion. But occasionally Mrs James would see through my little ruse. And if I saw her wiping her hands in her apron I knew that I was in for a sharp box on the ears. I soon learnt the need to be watchful.

I enjoyed my early schooldays very much. Indeed, the only task I hated was playing the violin. All I wanted was to be a farmer. Or failing that, an auctioneer. Carrying the violin in its case, therefore, was both a burden and a bore. My violin spent more time hidden in hedgerows than anywhere else. Having to carry it was in itself an irritation. But I had more reason than most to hide it as I owned the only brown carrying case. All the other pupils had black cases.

Despite my dislike of the violin I became quite adept as an instrumentalist, and performed in a few *gymanfas,* those religious singing festivals so beloved of the Welsh. I would play it by ear. I couldn't – and still can't – read music. And yes, I was happy at Llangwrddon school. It had everything. It even had its own small orchestra. And we were all expected to sing and perform recitations. All the very best of Welsh traditions were revered there.

The school's Christmas concert would be a special occasion. The orchestra would perform there, as well as a percussion band in which I played the triangle. Originally I played the drum. But playing as I did, over-zealously and most ineptly, I smashed a hole in the membrane. So I was demoted to the triangle. That was the one instrument that someone even as clumsy as I couldn't possibly destroy.

I well remember one Christmas concert when Sir Ifan ab Owen Edwards announced that he would be present. Sir Ifan was the founder of *Urdd Gobaith Cymru* – the Welsh League of Youth. This was – and is – a pacifist organization whose slogan is a swearing of allegiance to Wales, Fellowman and Christ. At that time, Sir Ifan's name meant very little to us children. We were only acquainted with local folk, people like William Evans Tanglogau, Dai Cnwc, Wil Ty Cam, Tom Treflys and so on. So when we heard that Sir Ifan ab Owen Edwards was to attend, we had no idea who this important man with the grand-sounding name was.

But attend he did, and looking back, that in itself indicates the high standards we were attaining. I remember Mrs Wilson running full pelt up from Will Woodward's shop and shouting at the headmistress: 'Mrs. Andrews! Mrs. Andrews! Have you heard? Sir Ifan ab Owen Edwards is coming to your concert tonight!'

We, the children, stood there stunned. Not to say a little bemused. Who was this man who was coming to visit us? And I remember asking Meurig Brynbwa: 'Tell me, who is this Sir Ifan ab Owen Edwards?'

'Damn, I've no idea,' he answered. 'He's probably someone important from the army.'

No matter, Sir Ifan came. And I can remember him addressing us at the end of the concert. That memory is something that will always remain with me.

I would walk to school – a good mile from Ty'n Cefen,

where I lived with Uncle Morgan and Aunty Hannah. The walk from home every morning was no problem. It was all downhill. That's why I was never given a bicycle. On a bike I would have been able to make it in a matter of a few minutes. But pushing it back uphill in the late afternoon would take a good two hours. So I walked.

This was a time when road-men were still seen here and there. And I truly believe that Wales has suffered from the demise of these council workers, or lengthsmen. They would look after their own patch meticulously. For one thing they would keep the water channels clear and running. Today, following one good shower, the roads overflow with water.

These road-men were characters, especially in our eyes. We would often linger with them and listen to their stories. Mrs Andrews gave me a good talking-to one day because I was late arriving in school. I had loitered too long listening to William Williams, Chapel House – he was our lengthsman – telling me tales which were, as always, laced liberally with white lies. Incidentally, I still believe that I learnt more on my way to and from school than I ever did in the classroom. I had more faith in William Williams's roadside sermons than I had in lessons.

Because of my regular chats with the road-man I was often late for school. And on this particular day, Mrs Andrews gave me an ultimatum. 'If you are late tomorrow, David John, it will be the cane for you.'

The following morning, arriving late, of course, I tried to sneak in quietly while the other children were reciting their morning prayers, their backs to the door. But she spotted me.

'Come here, David John,' she sternly ordered me. The children hadn't even had time to utter their Amen. 'Now then, hold your hand out. Wasting time talking to William Williams again, no doubt.'

'No, honestly, Miss,' I answered. 'This time it was William Williams talking to me.' Luckily for me she accepted the joke. And I saved myself from my first taste of the cane. But it was merely a postponement.

Yes, I would walk to school apart from those days when the rain was intolerable. Then a neighbour, Lewis Davies, Maesbeidiog, would give me a lift. His daughter, Olwen, was the same age as Trefor. She is now a farmer's wife in Ffair-rhos.

Lewis Davies differed from all the other neighbours. He would change his car every year. He kept his tractor – a two-seater David Brown – for years. But he would change his car regularly. I recall him once buying a Triumph Mayflower. It was a square car that looked like a large mustard box on wheels. Then he bought a Standard Vanguard.

On New Year's morning I would, with some of the other children, go around the area collecting *Calennig*. We would wish the neighbours a Happy New Year. And they would respond by giving us money. I would receive sixpence here, seven pence there, and sometimes as much as a half-crown. Olwen Maesbeidiog would be one of the gang. And it was at Maesbeidiog at around 3.30 in the afternoon that we would end up in order to count and share our spoils. Before leaving, we would all enjoy a cup of tea and an apple.

An important part of school life would be the annual outings, which were a natural extension of the curriculum. At springtime we would visit Banc Rhos y Garreg or Cnwc y Barcud. We would leave after dinner with Mrs Andrews leading and Miss Williams assisting. We would dote on the bluebells and other wild flowers and spend the afternoon playing in the open air. A trip to Disneyland would fade in comparison. The smell of those bluebells still linger. The gambolling newborn lambs were a sight to behold. And seeing a prancing foal would be very heaven.

Then came the summer outing, our annual school trip. It would mean an early dinner and off on the bus to Borth. We would go around through Llandre along the main road and back over the top to Clarach. In Borth itself we would spend the afternoon on the prom. Then, before leaving, we enjoyed a feast of fish and chips in the little cafe by the beach. I think the old place is still there.

Miss Williams had been born in Borth, so we would stop on the hill above the village so that we could see clearly the places which had been important to her as a child. And poor Miss Williams! We would bombard her with questions. Where had she attended school? What was school life like when she was our age? The questions would be never-ending.

As well as attending the primary school, I also went to Sunday School. This was something all the children did. In my class at Tabor, I was one of fifteen children. Miss Evans Felingwm, a very dear lady, was our teacher. She was a spinster and kept the small Felin Gwm shop. A diminutive woman, she would bring us sweets every Sunday, and we all thought the world of her.

The class was mainly made up of girls. The only boys amongst them were Dai Ty'n Llwyn, Gwilym Maesllyn and I. We then moved up a class where J.O. Evans, Gwar-caeau taught us. He was a local hero. As well as being a teacher he was also an accomplished singer who prepared us for the various vocal competitions in the annual *Cwrdd Bach*, a kind of mini-eisteddfod.

Half-way through Sunday School we would be questioned on our Biblical knowledge by the Superintendent. I once had the honour of holding that position, an honour which I still treasure. The fact that I wasn't a scholar by any stretch of the imagination makes that honour doubly important to me.

The questioning would be done by the visiting preacher. And whoever that preacher happened to be, he was always amazed at our knowledge of the Bible. We all had ready answers. No matter how complicated, how intricate the question, we would never fail, never falter. Why? Well, it certainly wasn't because of any great knowledge on our part. The truth is that J.O. Evans would furtively whisper the answers in our ears. And to ensure that we would comply with his harmless little scheme he would reward us later with sweets. Over the years he must have bought us tons of Bluebird Toffee as an innocent bribe. Gwilym Maesllyn would often say: 'It's worth answering the questions so we can have the *Deryn Glas.*' That was his way, in Welsh, of translating Bluebird.

Sometimes we would visit the local shop and attempt to buy the very sweets that J.O. would hand out to us. We would ask Jane behind the counter for a quarter of *Deryn Glas.* But it took her years to realize what we were asking for.

Tabor chapel was about a mile-and-a-half away from Ty'n Cefen. And Evans Tanglogau would pick up Trefor and me in his car. I well remember the little car. It was the first-ever Ford to be seen in the area. I can even recall its number, JXP 99. In the car, with Evans driving, William Howells Panteg would sit in the front passenger seat. And in the back would be crammed Olwen Maesbeidiog, my

28

brother Trefor and I. And, often adding to the crush, would be Leis Cornel – and Leis took up quite some room.

On Pengelli Hill the groaning, spluttering car would just about make it to the brow. An extra ounce in weight – if Leis, for instance, had happened to bring her handbag along – then one of us would have had to walk. And now and then, this would actually happen. Some of us – Trefor and I more often than not – would have to get out and walk the rest of the hill. The car would then continue and wait for us at the top. But we didn't mind. And we knew exactly, to the tick, when we should be out on the road waiting for the old JXP 99.

Even as a child, having returned from Sunday School, there would be various chores awaiting me at home. I was taught early how to milk the cows by hand. And by the time I was seven I could milk just as well as the next man. I would, of course, be confined to milking the docile cows.

I loved all this. But Trefor was a different matter. He did not take to farm work at all. Maybe – and this is a terrible thing to say about my own brother – maybe he was more of a loafer than I was. And I'm sure he would agree. But for myself, even before Uncle had asked me to do something, I would be there, ready at his heels. 'Defi, watch here. Defi, watch over there.' And I would obey immediately. He would sometimes leave for me a particular chore he could easily have completed himself. He seemed to want me to help him. He probably appreciated the company.

But Trefor was different. Although reluctant to involve himself he would, sometimes, be needed. Herding the cattle, for instance. Because Ty'n Cefen skirted the road, three people would often be needed to drive the cows – one behind, one in front and yet another one to turn them in

29

through the gate. Uncle would shout, 'Trefor, get down to open the gate of Cae Gwair and turn the cows in.' Trefor would answer, 'I'll go now, Uncle.' Then uncle would have to call again. 'Trefor, where are you?' And my brother would answer. 'I'll go now. After I've finished peeing.' He didn't want to go, of course. And Uncle would shake his head in despair and mutter, 'What in the world can I do with this boy. If it isn't pee-pee all day, then it's poo-poo. I'll have to send him back.'

He meant back to London, of course. But to me it sounded as if he wanted to return a faulty wireless battery.

But although he wasn't sent back, Trefor did return voluntarily to London later on, before he had finished school. And when I was 11 years old, I left as well. I don't mean that I left the farm. But I did leave the little village school to face life in the big school in Aberystwyth, Dinas Secondary School. And that's when I tried to persuade Dad to buy me a bicycle. When I needed new clothes or any other necessities he would send money from London to cover the cost. Uncle or Aunty would then take me to Daniel Thomas's shop in town to buy me a new set of clothing. But asking for a bike was another matter completely. I did my best to dupe Dad, but I failed.

'I have to leave early now to catch the bus,' I explained.

'I see. And where do you meet the bus?' Dad asked.

'Well, I have to walk either to Rhydroser or down to the village.'

Unfortunately, even though Dad lived far away he was only too aware of Llangwrddon's geography. And I never got the bike.

I started my first term at Dinas School on the very day that the new school opened its doors for the first time. The surrounding area has changed completely by now. But I remember the first five houses being built on what is now Waunfawr, which today is almost a town in itself. They were built by Cyril Jenkins, Penrhyn-coch. There was only one shop there then, Williams the Waun's shop. And with the opening of the school it must have been a godsend for the little store.

Dinas School was known as the Modern School, whereas Ardwyn School, the other secondary establishment in the town, was a Grammar School. Usually it was those that were less qualified educationally that attended Dinas. My attempts in the Eleven Plus examinations were not good enough to allow me to attend Ardwyn. But the truth of the matter is that I deliberately failed.

It was another road-man that sowed the seeds of suspicion in my mind. One morning, with the Eleven Plus examinations imminent, I stopped for the usual chat. And naturally, the subject of the impending exams was raised. And he then told me that his brother's children were attending Ardwyn School.

'Dai *bach*,' he said, 'you should see the amount of homework they get. Hell, Dai, don't go to Ardwyn or you'll end up a preacher.'

That was enough. I swore there and then that I would not go to Ardwyn. I would make sure I failed the Eleven Plus. When the exams came I wrote very little, concentrating instead on drawing pretty pictures and doodling. And when the morning of the results arrived I awaited with bated breath, just in case, as Mrs Andrews read out the list.

'Glenys Thomas – Ardwyn. Llywela Davies – Ardwyn.' And then, at last, she called my name. 'David John Jones – Dinas.' My relief was unbounded.

My memories of Dinas are rather mixed, especially so when I think back on the teachers. It is impossible for me to forget one in particular, Mair Evans, the Social Sciences teacher. She was one hell of a batterer. Compared to her, the Gestapo were amateurs! She made sure that I had more than my share of beatings. She was short in stature, but she would make up for that with her ability to mete out punishment.

Whenever I would upset her, which was often, she would order me, emphasising every word and pointing to the chair that faced her, 'Sit . . . down . . . there . . .' And as soon as I obeyed she would grab the form register, which had hard covers, and bring it down sharply time and time again on my head. Once, after tiring from her exertions, she ordered me off the chair and onto the floor so that she could enjoy more leverage.

The Social Science room was on the second floor. And should she stumble over someone's stray school bag lying in her path she would grab the offending satchel and hurl it out of the window. And whatever the weather, even if it was teeming with rain, you dared not retrieve the bag until the lesson was over.

One day she ordered me to leave the room for some minor transgression. Suddenly I heard the noise of the approaching headmaster. He would always wear crepe-soled shoes which, on the block flooring, made a sort of swishing noise. As the sound came ever nearer I knew I had to do something drastic to avoid six of the best. There on the windowsill next to me was the dreaded register. I quickly grabbed it and walked to meet the headmaster giving the impression that I was taking it to the secretary's office. He smiled at me and said, 'Nice to see you behaving for a change.'

'Thank you, sir,' I said as I scuttled past him.

On another occasion Tegwyn Rhosgoch and I had been given detention over the dinner hour. Our extra punishment was to sharpen pencils, two boxfuls in all. Tegwyn had never used the wall-fixed sharpener before so he asked me for guidance. Looking as serious as I could, I told him to push one end of the pencil in and to keep on turning the handle until the pencil came out the other end. Tegwyn believed me. But after mutilating three whole pencils he was puzzled. 'Damn,' he said, 'one of them should have come out by now.'

Realizing that I had been pulling his leg, he laughed. But now we had to hide the evidence. We cleared all the shavings and resumed sharpening the remaining pencils and returned them to their boxes. But we had reckoned without Miss Evans's built-in suspicions. We did not know that she had counted the pencils before leaving us. She found them three short. She started rifling through our pockets giving us a swipe across the head for every pocket. Then she started on our satchels. I thought that honesty was the best policy, so I confessed everything. And now came the father and mother of a beating. She tired so much from her exertions that she transferred the register to Tegwyn and ordered him to continue with the beating.

'But I can't,' Tegwyn protested, 'he's my friend.'

She then turned on Tegwyn. 'If you don't do it, then I'll start beating you.'

Tegwyn had no alternative but to beat me by proxy. He hit me once. But I must say that it was just a tickle compared to Miss Evans's beatings.

Not only was Tegwyn a good friend, he was quite a character as well. Once we were both given four hundred lines as punishment for yet another misdemeanour. I laboriously completed mine. Tegwyn, however, got off. He arrived at school the following day without his lines. But he presented half a hundredweight of potatoes to the teacher.

And once, in the middle of an English lesson, old Hughes English had to leave us to fetch a book from the storeroom. And Tegwyn took advantage of his absence to make mischief. Hughes returned and caught him at it.

'Tegwyn Lewis, shouting as usual,' said Hughes. 'Now, quickly, boy, what is the plural of horse?'

And quick as a flash, Tegwyn answered, 'Horsen, sir.'

Fortunately, we had some excellent teachers. There was Jones Woodwork, for instance. His father was a carpenter in Bethania, and was a local poet of note who once immortalized the Corgi in verse. And it was through J.E. Jones that we got our own back on Miss Evans. Every corridor had its own toilet, and the toilet in her corridor had run out of toilet paper. The nearest corridor was where the wood- and metal-work shops were located. In she stormed one day, and in front of the whole class she asked Jones, 'Have you any toilet paper, J.E.?'

'No, Mair,' he answered. 'But in our department we have plenty of sandpaper. Will that do?'

She left, her face a deep shade of red, to hoots of laughter.

Next door to the woodwork room was the metalwork room. The teacher there was T.R. Jones, who was a deacon at Blaenplwyf chapel. The first object I ever fashioned there was a poker. And I suppose you could say that I've been poking around minding other people's business ever since.

Jones Maths was another favourite. He would often ask me to help him clear up after lessons. He, at least, showed some interest in me. Another one was Dai Griffiths, the music teacher. There was one pupil in class who couldn't hit the *doh*. I slyly stuck a pin in his rear and he shouted out, 'Aw!'. 'No, no,' said Griffiths, 'it's *doh* I asked for.'

The Welsh teacher was W.R. Edwards, known to all as Jac y Bog. He once persuaded me to buy a copy of the Welsh comic *Hwyl* on the pretext that my name appeared in it. There was a cat and mouse cartoon in it, the cat being Tomi Puw and the mouse was named Defi John. My full name, by the way, is David John Jones. Dad would refer to me as Dai. But to Uncle Moc I would be Defi. And in school I was Defi John.

Another teacher whom I respected was T.G. Jones, or Tomi Penuwch. One day I had not completed my homework and I saw Tomi approaching. I knew that I would have to somehow distract him from inspecting my homework book. And there and then I had a brainwave.

'Mr. Jones,' I said, 'I spotted eight foxes last night, all standing in a row beneath the breast of the hill. And I took a photograph of them.'

'Well, well, that's interesting,' said Tomi. 'Will you bring the photograph to show me when it's been developed?'

'Yes, of course.'

There was no photograph. There hadn't been any foxes, come to that. But the ruse worked.

I continued playing the violin and became a member of the school orchestra. We would perform every morning at Assembly and the musicians included as many as three of us from Llangwrddon. There was Dai Ty'n Llwyn, Brinli Pengaer and myself.

And here, I should refer to Edwin Andrews, originally from the Rhondda. He was a peripatetic music teacher and was a genius with the bow. He had a remarkable left-hand technique. He was able to tempt an unusual tremolo from the instrument. His Welsh was rather ragged but his music was pure magic.

'You learn to play first,' he would advise me. 'Then you can tremble.'

Edwin was married to my ex-headmistress, Mrs Andrews. She was honoured with the MBE for her great service to her locality, a rare accolade in those days. But I would like to think that her husband contributed much to the decision to thus honour his wife.

Edwin Andrews introduced us gradually to music. He did not ram it down our throats. He made us feel that we were doing something special. And it was to his credit that he was able to form an orchestra that included farmers' children, whose calloused hands were more used to toil than caressing musical instruments.

In subjects like arithmetic I was as thick as two short planks. It was only from frequenting the local marts with Uncle that I picked up a knowledge of figures. Soon I was able to estimate the price of lambs as easily and as quickly as Uncle himself. I didn't need a Ready Reckoner.

I left school at fifteen, although I must confess that my attendance during the previous year had been sporadic. Looking back, I wasn't happy at Dinas. Not that I attach any blame to the school. It was my own mischievousness that led me to trouble. I must have appeared in front of the headmaster daily. And when I attended on my last day I told him that he would surely miss me. 'Why do you say that?' he asked. 'Well,' I said, 'I have been very faithful to you. After all, I came to visit you every day.'

Despite the natural rivalry between town and country there was little conflict between us and the town children in school. There were differences. We would say 'Panparce', while they would pronounce it 'Penpaki'. Anyway, some of the townies, pupils like Dai Rees and Goronwy Edwards had rural roots. And they would often visit their grandparents' farms. They therefore knew our ways.

Most of the conflict would occur outside school – and more often than not at the annual town fairs every November. I was never involved in a fracas. I wasn't much of a fighter, but damn, I could run.

All I had ever looked forward to while at school, from the very first day, was the minute when I would be able to leave. And in my case there were many last days; as I would often swear that I would never go back. But the official last day duly arrived and I could have shouted with joy. In fact, I think I did. On that last day the headmaster predicted that four of us, Tegwyn Rhosgoch, Meirion Jones, Richard Mathews and I would never amount to much. But I'm glad to say that we've all done pretty well – in fact, rather better than the headmaster himself ever did.

A batch of us had left Llangwrddon for Dinas at the same time, Meurig Brynbwa, Dai Ty'n Llwyn and I amongst them. Strangely enough, all three of us celebrated our birthdays during the same month. And having returned to school following what we would refer to as the potato holidays, all the other pupils would sing 'Happy Birthday' to us. I still recall the various dates: Dai on the 8th of October, Meurig on the 28th and myself on the 18th, all of us within ten days of each other.

Leaving Llangwrddon with us had been Jean Bryngwyn, Mair Langors, Llywela Treflys, Sheila Penbryn, Ann Cornel and Glenys Penbont. That was quite a loss to a small rural school.

Yes, I loved every minute at Llangwrddon school. And despite Miss Evans, strange as it may seem, I harbour some fond memories of Dinas as well. I firmly believe that all of us country children should have been sent there rather than to the grammar school. After all, there is little purpose in over-educating country children, is there?

3

Home-grown Heroes

Llangwrddon is a small village which straddles the river Wyre. And I always pronounce it Llangwrddon. Its official name, Llangwyryfon, means nothing to me. In the same way, I will never say Llanfihangel. To me it will always be Llaningel.

During those school years at Dinas nine or ten of us would congregate on the bridge every morning to await the school bus. Why there, I don't know. The village telephone kiosk, its only telephone kiosk, stood nearby. Sometimes we would play tricks on the villagers. The kiosk had no light at that time. So, during the dark evenings we would round up some of the village cats, up to a dozen at a time, and imprison them in the kiosk. When someone happened to open the kiosk door to make a call, all hell would break loose. Mind you, I would never be involved in actually catching the cats. I would merely hold the door open as I have always been terrified of cats.

This may sound strange of someone who, as a farmer, should be completely at ease with creatures of the feline variety. But there lies a simple explanation behind my terror of cats. When I was a child and had just started school, I was confined to bed with flu. My brother Trefor and Olwen Maesbeidiog came into the bedroom to keep me company. And of course, it was Trefor who had the bright idea of smuggling in a cat behind his back. Before I knew what was happening he threw the creature onto the bed. The cat panicked and I grabbed it. But I grabbed it so hard that it left behind on the bed something that it shouldn't have. The result of all this was that I, in blind terror, chucked the poor creature out of the window. But as a consequence I have always been scared of cats.

Llangwrddon is a delightful village. Whichever road you take out of it you have to climb a hill. Rhiw'r Eglwys – Church Hill – leads up past the cemetery. Then there is Rhiw Tan'rallt, or Rhiw Capel Bach. Rhiw Ficrej, or Vicarage Hill leads out towards the town and then there's Rhiw Carnau. Why Rhiw Carnau? Well, *carnau* means hooves and along that road lie some of the larger farms whose horses would often need shoeing at the local smithy. Perhaps that is the explanation.

There were some natural meeting-places in the village. There would be the mill, the carpenter's shop, the smithy. And within them the chatting and gossiping in Welsh would be as natural a part of everyday life as the sounds of the craftsmen themselves while they worked. Then we had the *Cwrdd Bach*, which means Small Meeting, where we took part in singing and recitation competitions. That was a prime event in the locality. For weeks leading up to it there would be rehearsals with choirs, octets, quartets, duets and individual soloists honing their talents. It was at the *Cwrdd Bach* that I first faced an audience, in the *solo twps* competition, one which was especially reserved for those who had never won before.

The adjudicators would be steeped in Welsh culture, having been through the competitive mill themselves. One year we had John Bryngalem from Bwlch-llan and Mair

Meiarth adjudicating. They were so impressed that they invited us all back to compete at Bwlch-llan against the pick of the locals in that area. So it was Tabor versus Bwlch-llan, a true local derby.

One of my favourite adjudicators was E.D. Jones, Tregaron, known to all and sundry as Jonesy Bach, not because he was related to Johann Sebastian but because he was small. Jonesy was a genius. And although the language of the meeting would be wholly Welsh – to us, speaking Welsh was as natural as breathing – Jonesy liked to turn to English when he wished to emphasize a point. Once, a local girl called Muriel had been among the singers competing. And off went Jonesy with his peroration. 'Muriel, I don't like . . .' We expected the worst as he strode back and forth along the stage his head up and his arms outstretched for dramatic effect. 'Muriel, I don't like your loud singing. But Muriel . . .' He now took off his spectacles. 'But Muriel, you're lovely when you're soft.'

One of the regular competitors was Dai Evans, a bachelor who lived with his spinster sister, Lil. He was known locally as Dai Cnwc, or Dai Cnwc y Barcud. Once he attempted to sing a hymn on the tune *Gwalchmai.* But he had trouble hitting the opening note. The first line was, '*Caned Nef a daear lawr . . .*', which means, 'Let all Heaven and earth sing . . .' Dai hit the first note, '*Caned . . .*' Too sharp. He tried again, '*Caned . . .*' This time he was too flat. The adjudicator was that lovely man, Dai Williams, Tregaron. He attempted to help Dai Cnwc by hitting the opening note himself. And Dai Williams pitched it perfectly. '*Caned . . .*' Dai Cnwc looked over his spectacles at Dai Williams and brought the house down by asking the adjudicator, 'Excuse me, but who's supposed to be singing this hymn? You or me?'

The village boasted two shops, New-bridge and the Commercial. And both these shops were, of course, natural meeting places. The Commercial, which doubled as the post office, still remains. New-bridge shop was kept by Wil Woodward. And naturally, to us, it was known as Shop Wil Woodward.

Wil was a great character and was one of my childhood heroes. As part of his shop he kept a small printing press. And he lived with Mrs Wilson. She was from Liverpool and, as innocent children, we couldn't understand how two people with different surnames could live together. Wil was a bachelor and had probably met Mrs Wilson while on one of his travels.

One of Wil's little idiosyncrasies was his smoking habit. He would always smoke Craven 'A'. I wasn't too happy with his choice of cigarettes as these had a logo sporting a black cat's head on the carton. But not only was Wil a heavy smoker, he was also an unconventional smoker. The cigarette would never leave his lower lip. There it would hang, swaying rhythmically like a pendulum while he talked. Many of the pearls of wisdom that, unlike his cigarette, fell from his lips, we would ignore. We were too engrossed in watching to listen. We were mesmerized by that swaying cigarette that seemed like a natural extension of his lower lip.

Wil was way ahead of his time. He was the village pioneer. It was Wil who bought the first-ever fridge in the neighourhood. One day, when we entered the shop, he welcomed us with the news that he would be selling ice cream the following evening. And he urged us to keep our money until we were on our way home from school when we could spend it on this new treat. I was so excited that I ordered an ice cream wafer in advance.

Throughout the following day our money was burning a hole in our pockets. We couldn't wait for classes to end. But in the meantime Wil must have had a problem with his fridge's thermostat. I got my wafer all right and I think it cost me sixpence. But all I found inside the wrapper was a runny white liquid between two biscuits. But I didn't mind. Every time I had money in my pocket I would spend it on Wil Woodward's ice cream.

It was in Wil Woodward's shop that I heard the story about Siw Penuwch. She always dressed colourfully and looked like a mobile rainbow. And wherever she went, her shoulder-bag would always be present. Siw sold milk, a mere single churn-full a day. During warm summer days it was quite a task to keep the milk cool, especially as the churn would stand for hours in the open air. Regularly, the previous day's milk would be returned with a red label tied to the churn's handle informing Siw that her milk had curdled. After a few days of this, Siw had suffered enough. Down she went to the creamery at Felin-fach.

Seeing her arrive, the staff who knew her immediately retreated. They realized that a storm was about to break. Rather than face her themselves they persuaded a newcomer, a young deputy manager, to confront her. He was only about 21 years old and looked even younger. But even worse than that to Siw was the fact that he couldn't speak Welsh. Siw dutifully stated her case. But in return she received a severe reprimand from the little official. He warned Siw that she would have to learn to produce untainted milk. Siw, who had been producing milk before this young upstart was sucking his dummy, could not take any more. She looked long and hard at this whipper-snapper with his collar and tie. And then she struck.

43

'Look here, my boy,' growled Siw, 'you may be brilliant at talking. But I want you to understand one thing. Make sure you fasten the safety-pins on your nappy, boy, because you're not going to shit on Siw.'

Stories like that were rife in Woodward's Shop. And it was there that I would spend my Saturday nights rather than going to Aberystwyth with my friends. I would sit there listening to the discussions. Ifan Williams Rhandir Ucha, Dewi Jones Ffynnon Wen, Dafydd Thomas Y Felin, Tom Davies Penglanowen and William Evans Tanglogau – they would all congregate there. Wil would never have enough chairs for them to sit on, so some of us would grab lemonade crates, upend them and utilise them as chairs. To a young lad like me, being allowed to listen to these local sages was bliss.

The first funeral I ever attended was Wil Woodward's. I was still a young boy, still attending school. And I'll never forget Wil Woodward's coffin being passed out through the window next to the shop doorway. And there I watched, thinking of the man who had bought the first fridge, who had sold me my very first ice cream. And now he was dead. Yes, Wil Woodward. A giant of a man.

People like Wil Woodward were my heroes. And among them were the brothers who lived at the mill, Joe and Stephen Y Felin. They were the best spitters I ever encountered. They had turned spitting into a fine art, especially Joe. You could nominate any target anywhere and Joe would hit it with a perfectly delivered gob of spit like a guided missile.

It was impossible to think of the village without also thinking of Joe and Stephen. It was at the mill that we would dip the sheep. We would drive the flock down the road from Mynydd Bach and immerse them in the millpond. It was an exceptionally deep pond but I swear that the brothers spat enough to fill it many times over.

They would both chew Ringers tobacco. One morning a gang of us children were wandering along the river-bank looking for otters when Stephen stopped to talk to us. As usual, he was chewing tobacco. He spat, and the spit accidentally landed in his sheepdog's eye. Off it went, howling and running around the village like a banshee. People must have thought that the deluge had returned. Joe duly arrived and asked Stephen why had he done such a terrible thing? 'Well,' said Stephen, 'I was aiming at the gate and missed.' And Joe squared up and showed his brother how to really do it. He pursed his lips and let go. And splat! He aimed his spit perfectly between two bars of the gate. Yes, Joe and Stephen. They could have won countless Welsh caps for spitting.

Then there was the village blacksmith, Dic y Gof. Not only was he the blacksmith, he also doubled as a postman. Whenever a horse was being shod in his smithy we would all congregate there. Famous stallions would pass through the village every spring on their way to the smithy. Mathrafal Frenin, Brenin Gwalia, Pentre Eirwen Comet, all of them kings that reigned supreme in the stallion world.

In Dic's garden in Aberdeuddwr there grew the sweetest apples this side of Eden. When we visited the smithy we would try our best to behave knowing that Dic would then give us an apple each. One afternoon, when Dic was away, a gang of us went scrumping in his garden. The forbidden fruit tasted even sweeter than the ones Dic gave us. Stolen apples, like stolen kisses, always seem to taste sweeter.

I would also visit the carpenter's shop where I would see

Edwin James making coffins, amongst the odds and ends. Edwin had his little idiosyncrasy. Whenever he had a cigarette he would never have matches. And whenever he had matches, he wouldn't have a cigarette. When he needed a light he would look around until he found someone who was puffing on a cigarette. He would then embrace the smoker with one arm and place the end of his own cigarette against the glowing end of his visitor's. Then, not only would he suck at his cigarette but he would also press hard leaving the unfortunate smoker's cigarette bent like a question mark.

Another local character was Mari Langors. She would always click her tongue with the regularity of a ticking clock. Sometimes I would meet her in the shop and would greet her, 'Hello, Mari. How are you today?' And Mari would answer, 'Click, click, click, click. Just you be careful, boy.'

One late evening Eirwyn Llaindelyn and I were walking along the road when we heard a clicking noise coming from over the hedge. 'An electric fence,' said Eirwyn. And we both decided, for a laugh, to climb over the fence and switch it off. But when we entered the field we heard a voice, 'Click, click. What do you think you're doing, you rascals?' Yes, it was Mari.

Someone who was always good for a laugh was Ned Jones, or Ned y Llain. Ned was a road-man who would often jest, telling us that he used his billhook as a razor every time he shaved in the morning. And he would demonstrate the technique, holding his nose with thumb and forefinger while drawing the billhook blade along his chin. And of course, we believed him.

Ned was always scared of thunder and lightning,

especially the lightning. Whenever he would be caught in a thunderstorm he would rest his head on the saddle of his bike and hide his face under his overcoat. This happened one afternoon as a local farmer was passing. Seeing Ned, he crept up to him stealthily and slapped him on the bottom and tiptoed away. 'Damn,' said Ned, 'that was a close one.'

Very few English people had discovered Llangwrddon in those days. As a result very little English was needed and this meant that many were monolingual. I remember Lisi Pengelli – I would visit Pengelli regularly to chat to Lisi and her brother Owen. For one thing they kept Speckle-faced sheep, a rarity at that time as most farmers kept Welsh sheep.

Once, having been helping Owen, I was invited in for tea. Lisi and Owen's cousin and her niece from London had called. They spoke no Welsh whatsoever. Lisi asked her cousin, in her best Sunday English, whether she was ready for her tea?

'Oh, yes,' her cousin answered, 'but be very careful. Make sure I have just a dash of sugar in the bottom of the cup. And I would like it very weak with just a spot of milk on top.'

There stood Lisi holding a teapot that was almost as big as a bucket. She looked her cousin straight in the eye and barked, 'Any particular speed from the teapot?'

Trefor's departure to London left me feeling rather lonely. Fortunately I had four cousins – three brothers and a sister – living in Brynchwith, Dad's old home. Islwyn, Trefor, Ceredig and Mair's parents were Uncle Dan and Aunty Jane. We were so close that we were more like brothers and sister than cousins. And that's how I still regard them.

Brynchwith was like a second home to me. Once when I

visited, Uncle and Aunty had gone to town leaving Islwyn, who had measles, in bed. There was no indoor toilet there so Islwyn had to use the pot that was kept under the bed. And by the time I arrived the pot was full.

Islwyn and I started playing with little plastic boats that came free with packets of Cornflakes. One of us had a brainwave. We started floating the little model boats in the chamber pot. Tiring of this game, Islwyn pushed the pot back under the bed. But he didn't push it far enough. While playing hide-and-seek he caught the edge of the pot with his foot and over it went. The bedroom floor was flooded. And worse, the pot's contents began seeping through the floorboards down to the kitchen. And there was Islwyn on his hands and knees trying to dry the bedroom floor while I was frantically cleaning the kitchen slabs with a mop and bucket before Uncle and Aunty arrived home.

Apart from my father and his brother, my Uncle Wil, all of Dad's family opted to stay in the immediate area. Their parents were John and Mari Jones, Brynchwith, a farming family through and through. I can vaguely recall Mam-gu Brynchwith, Dad's mother, tending an ailing chick. She had tucked it into an old sock in front of the fire so it could keep warm. That old open fireplace is still there together with the old-fashioned crane that lifted and held the old cast-iron kettles and cauldrons.

Ten children were raised in Brynchwith. Morgan was the eldest, then came William, John, Dick – my father – Daniel, David, Gilbert and the youngest, Trefor. Then there were Aunty Lisi and Aunty Jane. Uncle Trefor died when he was only 21. And strangely some of the others died at the age of 46. The last of the Brynchwith children died six years ago aged 85.

Aunty Lisi, by the way, became Bodo Lisi, Bodo being a colloquial name for an aunt. The reason for the change was my cousin Ceredig. When he was small he suffered from the stutters. And he found it easier to say Bodo than Aunty. Often, during an altercation with one or both of his parents he would threaten to leave and go to live with 'Bo-bo-bodo Lisi'.

Ceredig and I would often stay with Bodo Lisi and Uncle Jim at Penty Parc, Llanilar. They, like Uncle Moc and Aunty Hannah, were childless and were glad to have us there. Uncle Jim was a cowman on the Castle Hill estate. On Sundays he would take us to Waun Gron to see the cattle and sheep. Then, back to Castle Hill to see the Ayreshires being milked. Castle Hill was huge compared to Ty'n Cefen and we found all sorts of adventures there.

Were I to visit Penty Parc and Bodo Lisi was away I would write in chalk on the slate doorstep, a slab of blue stone, to inform her that I'd called. A piece of chalk was always hidden under the window sill, and this was a kind of secret arrangement between Ceredig and I and Bodo Lisi. One day Ceredig, when he was about five years old, called at Penty Parc only to find that Bodo was away. So he carefully wrote on the stone slab, 'Ceredig has b-b-b-been here.' Yes, he wrote exactly as he spoke, with a stutter.

But to return to Brynchwith. I would often visit there as a child, and as the place did not boast a toilet I was once caught short badly. We were playing outside when I felt I had to go. And to make things worse, it wasn't number one I wanted to do but number two. What an experience it was! Wanting to go, wanting desperately to go, but the others not leaving me alone. They pretended to go away but instead they hid. And when I thought they had gone, I could hear

49

them sniggering from behind the bushes. Of course, it became a calamity. And the dreaded disaster struck. I remember Aunty Jane having to clean me. She stood me on a copy of the *Welsh Gazette* in front of the fire. But the biggest joke of all to the others was the fact that there wasn't a spare pair of underpants in the house. I had to make do instead with a pair of Mair's blue knickers while my clothes were being washed.

Toilets then, at best, were rudimentary. In school there were no locks on the doors. When someone wanted to go he would take a friend with him to stand guard outside. And if it rained then that friend would have to shelter in the same toilet. But believe you me, it was much healthier outside.

All Dad's family, apart from himself and Uncle Wil, became farmers. Uncle John, who died when he was 46, farmed Mynydd Brith, Blaenpennal. Uncle Dai farmed Pen-rhiw, and I would spend much of my time with him. He was quite a hero in my eyes. Uncle Dai had two daughters, Eirian, who is married to Aled Wyn Williams, the vicar of Llanddewi Brefi, and Evelyn, who married Islwyn Morgan, Nant y Berws, the former headmaster of Pontrhydfendigaid school.

Uncle Dai was very much involved with market gardening and I would travel with him on the tractor when he ferried loads of vegetables to town. Potatoes, carrots, beetroot – he would grow all sorts of vegetables. Pen-rhiw was only about four miles from town and we would deliver the vegetables in sacks just as the shops opened in the morning.

Another journey I would always look forward to was the annual visit to the Devil's Bridge sheep sale every summer. Once I travelled with William Jones, Ty'n Llwyn and old

Huw Williams, Pant y Barwn. In the back was Dai, William Jones's son, his sister Lisa and myself. I felt so privileged to be able to listen to two experts, William and Huw, discussing sheep. I have always been drawn towards people like these. Even when I was a child in the middle of a game or escapade I would leave my friends to join any informal gathering of some of the village elders. I found them so original in their ways, so humorous in their deliberations. Many of their quaint sayings have remained with me and they have become part of my own vocabulary.

Bodo Lisi, like Uncle John, died when she was 46 years old. Then Aunty Jane died at the same age. She was a spinster who stayed on in Brynchwith and I have little recollection of her. All that I can recall is that she was on the large side.

All the Brynchwith family were large. They were big and strong. The only exceptions were Dad and Uncle Morgan. But one characteristic that they all shared was their corpulence. Uncle Gilbert was probably the thinnest, but all the others could boast large paunches. I once heard someone teasing Uncle Moc about the size of his paunch. 'Morgan *bach*, what are you doing with such a large belly?' Uncle answered with a smile, 'There's nothing wrong with having a large belly. Just you remember this, all the big fish are found underneath the river-bank.' And I would tend to agree with him.

It would be impossible not to include Uncle Moc among my childhood heroes. He was very quick with his answers. He would buy his coal from Llanrhystud Road, the name that the railway company gave to Llanfarian Station. All his neighbours bought coal from the Co-op but the Llanrhystud Road merchant was related somehow or other to Aunty

Hannah. So we bought the coal from him. One of the neighbours asked Uncle one day, 'What's the coal like, Moc?' 'Wonderful coal,' he replied. 'It may well be good coal,' said the neighbour. 'But is it easy to light? That's the test for really good coal.' 'This coal lights so well that you have to throw it on the fire from a distance,' he answered, 'otherwise the shovel will catch fire.'

He was always sharp with his answers. Lewis Maesbeidiog called one threshing day and noted that the sheaves had run pretty low. Uncle was well known as a good feeder. 'You've been pretty free with your sheaves, Moc,' he said. 'After all, it's still only October.' Lewis only kept a few milking cows and Uncle answered, 'Many mouths will eat much, my boy.'

The Brynchwith family were horse people through and through. My grandfather kept the famous Wyre Stud where he bred some notable horses, Wyre Star and Wyre Princess among them. They would take the honours in all the surrounding shows. The stud was named after the river Wyre, of course. And the Welsh cob, I'm pleased to say, is now established worldwide.

One of my greatest heroes was Moc Tanglogau. I would call round to see him at every available opportunity to help him pick potatoes, swedes and mangolds. I would also help at the shearing and on threshing days. And Moc was my role model.

He was younger than most farmers in the area and that was probably one of the reasons that I took to him so readily – that, and the fact that he looked like a drover with his yellow coat and his blackthorn stick. He also had a great interest in sheepdogs.

And it was at Tanglogau that one of the highlights of my

youth occurred, the arrival of the first-ever Friesian cow to the area. She came – and I'll never forget the name as long as I live – from the Kenneth Beeston Farms in Shropshire. Moc had told me that she would arrive from England in a huge cattle truck sometime before Sunday. And I couldn't wait for the lorry to arrive.

Then, at milking time one evening, I heard the rumbling sound of a heavy lorry. I ran out and saw it approaching. It filled the road and had lights everywhere like a huge mobile Christmas tree. And as it neared I was able to read the magic words, Kenneth Beeston Farms on its cab.

Back I ran to the cowshed and shouted to Uncle Morgan, 'I'm off to Tanglogau. The Friesian has arrived.' I ran and followed the lorry for part of the way then I took a shortcut through Cae Llwybyr and up through Cae Ddwygraig and I was at Tanglogau before the lorry to break the news to Moc that the Friesian was on her way. Moc was halfway through milking and all he said was, 'Well, well, and there's me thinking you were afraid of the dark. And that's when it hit me. I had always been scared of the dark, as scared as I was of cats. But in the excitement I had forgotten my terror.

The Friesian was led out of the lorry. And what a sight! One night, as Moc was milking her, I suddenly remembered something I had seen in a brochure that had arrived with the milk cheque. It was a picture of a bull, a grand looking bull. His name was Fennington Max Duplicate. Still completely lost in the excitement I told Moc, 'Do you know what you should give this cow? That new bull that the *A.I.* have got, Dennington Max Duplicate.'

'If you say so, Dai *bach*,' he answered patiently, 'then she'll have the Duplicate, no doubt.'

I don't know whether she got the Duplicate, but I know for a fact that there will never be a duplicate of Moc Tanglogau. Neither will there ever be a duplicate of Llangwrddon, the neighbourhood that shaped me and made me what I am today.

4

The Young Farmer

Leaving Dinas School at the Christmas break when I was fifteen was one of the greatest feelings of my life. It was an uplifting experience, especially after the holidays when all the others were going back to school. From the farmyard I watched the school bus climb the hill past the Vicarage realizing that I now had every right not to be on it.

My wage was £2 a week. And whatever Uncle Morgan bought for me he would jot it down in his little notebook and subtract it from my wages. Then Dad, at the end of the month, would make up the difference.

Sometime in October, before I had left school, I had been up to London to visit the Dairy Show. That gave me the opportunity to buy new clothes which I could wear after work when I would frequent the Young Farmers' Club meetings and various other local events. It was a lovely feeling to be able to cast aside my old school clothes, the blazer and grey trousers, the cap and the grey shirt and the yellow tie never to wear them again. I consigned them all to the rubbish bin.

Up in London, mother bought me a sports coat. And I felt quite the lad when I returned home. That night, a Thursday night, there was a concert held at Tabor chapel organized by the Young Farmers. I had been elected to propose the vote of thanks at the end, and I had prepared for the occasion for days going over the words again and again in the mirror.

My next acquisition was more practical. I needed proper working clothes. And again I was told to go to London to buy them. I knew that it meant Dad taking me to the Army and Navy Stores. But I was rather particular. I wanted proper farm clothes as I felt now that I was a real farmer. So the only item I bought in London was a beret: it made me look like a Breton onion seller.

So I persuaded my father to give me money towards the clothes. And I felt great when I was able to make my own choice. They were supplied by a travelling salesman who drove a van for J W Davies, Lampeter. I bought corduroy trousers, a shirt, a red neckerchief and a blue coat.

Next I needed a pair of strong boots. I bought those from Dai Pugh from Stag's Head who was a member of a travelling troupe that toured the county entertaining the various neighbourhoods. The troupe was made up of members of one family who were extremely versatile.

Now I had all the tackle and I really felt now that I was quite a man. I had been well-acquainted with farm work since I was about twelve years old. We had one farm-hand, Dai Royal Oak, Llanrhystud. Another man who was much older, Tom Davies, or Tom Troed-foel would help out. Were it not for going to chapel on Sunday, Tom would seldom bother to wash or shave. A neighbour, Joe Brynbeidiog would call every Monday to collect the Sunday paper, *The People,* after we had finished with it. Joe would always be dressed in breeches and leggings and had a bushy moustache just like Jimmy Edwards.

One Monday when Joe dropped in, an official from the National Insurance office also called to check on Tom's

National Health stamp payments. Upon seeing Joe he asked him if Mr Davies was anywhere around. Tom, as it happened, was cleaning the pigsty. 'Yes, he's around. He's cleaning under the pigs,' said Joe, adding, 'and by the way, Mr Davies is the one with the cap.'

Joe was also involved on another occasion when a Mr Lovell from somewhere in England had come to live at Llwynbedw. Mr Lovell was going to perform miracles, it seemed. As a stranger and a newcomer, his aim in life was to educate the village idiots. He must have felt like a missionary. Early February one year, Lovell decided to plough ley land. And as Lovell ploughed, his son-in-law planted potatoes under the turfs, this despite the fact that it was freezing hard. This puzzled Joe immensely so over he went to the field to ask Lovell what in the world was going on?

'Well,' said Lovell, 'I'm planting potatoes.'

'Damn,' said Joe, 'don't you realize that it's only early February?'

'Yes,' answered Lovell. 'Back in England I've seen farmers get eighteen tons to the acre by doing this.'

And quick as a flash, Joe answered, 'Eighteen tons? You'll be bloody lucky to get eighteen potatoes here.'

Anyway, having left school I started working full-time after Christmas that year. It was deep winter, and all the cattle were tethered in the cowshed. We didn't have running water there then and we had to do all the milking by hand. Before long, however, a milking machine was installed, consisting of two Alpha-Laval units.

But during those early days we had to turn the cattle out to water every day. There was a running stream alongside the road and the cows were allowed to walk down to drink there two by two. As two cows left, we would take advantage of their absence to clean out their stalls before milking. It meant brushing the stalls thoroughly, scraping the mangers clean and washing out the muck from behind the stalls. Then we would spread clean, dry straw over the cubicle floors. It worked well. As two cows returned from the stream to their stalls, two others would leave for water.

I would also feed the cows, filling their mangers with chaff mixed with pulped mangolds or swedes combined with treacle, oatmeal and bran. All the ingredients had to be thoroughly mixed and carried in buckets. Those cows which had just calved were treated to a further addition of gruel so that we could get the best out of them.

While I enjoyed the work, it was hard going, especially at wintertime. Mucking out with a pitchfork and a wheelbarrow in the cold was no joke. No sign of a muck-loader in those days. Every Saturday morning I would tidy the dung heap having daily pushed the barrow along a narrow plank and emptied it dozens of times. Tidying meant raising the plank and squaring off the heap. I would leave it as square as a hayrick. Cattle dung was much drier in those days and was easier to deal with than the manure you see nowadays. Today it runs like gravy. Cows in the old days would defecate like donkeys.

A nightly task, whatever the weather, was to thoroughly wash the wheelbarrow and place it, handles up, against the cowshed wall. Then I would wash the brush and pitchfork. Once a week I would brush out the farmyard, and since I was the youngest, I would carry out the duties of the junior farmhand. The rest of the work was carried out by Dai and Tom. And Uncle, of course.

Dai owned a motorbike, a BSA 250. And I lost my head

completely over it. He had bought it in Gwalia Garage, Aberystwyth and its registration was FEJ something-or-other. One day I was sitting astride the motorbike, which was on its stand in the barn while Dai and Tom were out fencing or trimming hedges. I was now Geoff Duke. I was the world champion racing motorcyclist. I turned the handlebars back and forth and imitated the sound of the engine. Gradually I got more daring and I kick-started the bike. To my horror the engine fired. I was so surprised that I sat back and the bike, which was in gear, sprang forward like a stallion into the middle of the chaff. Hell, I was frightened. I'll never forget that moment. But I never touched that motorbike again.

We kept a second farm called Troed y Foel, which was further up the mountain in Trefenter. I would often ride there on Prince, the black pony with the two sheepdogs, Scott and Prince, as company. On the way I couldn't resist loitering here and there for a gossip: but I would pass Maesbeidiog. There was no point in stopping as they would all be out working in the fields. So I would continue on to Pant Teg to see Will and Cato. There I would linger with them for a while before moving on. No-one was to be seen at Llwynbedw. And I would hurry past Gwar Nant – Evan Bailey always kept some fierce dogs and Prince would prick up his ears as he trotted past.

We would go up along Llwynbedw Hill, where on the crest stood Penllwyn Bedw, the house on the right and the out-buildings on the left. On the little homestead, two brothers and a sister kept three cows. Catrin was a spinster and her brother Tom worked as a farmhand in Ty Nant with Mati. The other brother, Jâms, lived at home. The chatting here would last quite a while with Prince grazing the grassy edge of the road while Catrin, Jâms and I put the world in its place.

A tall hedge grew in front of the house, high above the road, and I would often wonder what the consequences would be should Jâms lose his balance and fall straight through that hedge. No doubt he would have landed headlong on the road. But Jâms, oblivious of any danger, would always lean towards the hedge. And he would laugh in a peculiar way, the kind of 'hi-hi-ha-ha-ho-ho-hi-hi' that a nightjar made.

As for Catrin, an exploding bomb beneath her feet would barely move her. She was a calm woman who spoke slowly and measuredly. But she, like her brother, always enjoyed a chat.

Up I would continue towards Bethel, or Trefenter to give the village its official name. Bethel was the name of the chapel. Here again I would linger to talk to Beti and Neli Ty'n Ddraenen and old Edwin Rowlands. Edwin had been a singer of note who had boasted a sonorous bass voice. And he would often reminisce about the old times when he would sing eisteddfodic pieces like *The Inchcape Bell, Balthasar* and *Niagara*.

Then it would be on again towards Maes-yr-Haf where Miss Evans lived. It would be rare for her to make an appearance, but when she did she would always be a picture of refinement with her perfect sense of dress and her snow-white hair. The only day of the year I could be certain of seeing her was New Year's Day. She could also be seen on a few sunny summer days.

On yet again I would go. And in Waun Gron I would see Mari. And then the Rowlands family at Pendre. These were a family of butchers and Ianto Rowlands was the king of them all. He loved to joke with us youngsters. He once told me of a lorry driver who had knocked on his door to ask for directions. This man's arms, said Ianto, were covered with tattoos. But Ianto had seen better. When he was in the army, said Ianto, he had seen a soldier taking a bath. And this soldier was tattooed with a hunting scene with the horses and their riders on his shoulders and the hounds running down the small of his back. 'And damn it,' said Ianto, 'he had a fox's tail disappearing up his arse.'

Hours after starting my journey I would arrive at Troed y Foel. And by the time I had fed the cattle and sheep it would be time for me to return.

Socially there was very little to do for a lad like me. It was an unwritten rule of Uncle and Aunty that I should be home by ten every night. But I was allowed to stay late on Thursday nights at the Young Farmers' Club meeting. These meetings would start at eight. And there was one thing you could always say about the Llangwrddon members – they would be in no hurry to go home. The meetings were held at the Church Hall, which was looked after by Dick and Blanche Rhosgoch. There would always be a fire lit for us. And I swear that Dick and Blanche, during the winter months, would put a barrow-load of coal on the fire. And there was hardly any point in leaving until the fire had burnt itself out. And because the coal fire had been set around a substantial block of oak, we would stay there until the early hours of the morning.

Despite the fact that the meetings were well attended, few of us were old enough to take part in the various competitions that the YFC movement provided. But the fact that we had older members meant that speakers of note would attend to address us. I can well remember Llwyd o'r

Bryn addressing us on more than one occasion. He was a poet, a wit and a countryman through and through. And I believe that he had a lot to do with the fact that I became so attached to country ways and customs. He was every inch the proud, cultured peasant, and lived in Cefnddwysarn near Bala. And as for his anecdotes, I could never hear enough. At that time he was a contributor to the *Welsh Farm News*.

Bob Owen Croesor also visited us. An amateur historian and genealogist he was a small, short-tempered, quixotic man who would always be puffing on a Woodbine. He was a great shouter. At the time it was easy to forget that people like these were among the foremost of Welsh raconteurs.

Llwyd o'r Bryn's real name was Bob Lloyd. Then there was Bob Owen. And there was a third, Bob Roberts, Tai'r Felin. They were known far and wide as The Three Bobs. The only one of the three I never got to meet was Bob Roberts. He was a folk singer of note from Frongoch near Bala and I would have given anything to have met him. Every time I look at a photograph of my grandfather on my father's side, it reminds me of Bob Tai'r Felin.

The lateness of the YFC meeting held one great disadvantage. I was scared of the dark. I would always arrange for someone to pick me up on my way to the Club, usually Glyn Penglanowen. But going home was the problem. I could never leave before the others. No one would accompany me because of the simple fact that it would be far too early. Sometimes, if there was no one left to give me a lift I would walk home in the company of Leis, who worked as a maid at Penglanowen. Leis thought nothing of walking home late in the dark. Neither did Eileen, her successor.

Though we were a small club membership-wise, we

would have to take part in all sorts of activities. There was the public-speaking competition, the quiz, the one-act play, the cattle and sheep judging in the annual rally. Over the years, I was privileged to take part in all these activities, and later, to compete in the movement's eisteddfod.

Local people would only be too ready with their help in preparing for the various competitions. And one who was especially helpful was Dr Richard Phillips, Argoed. Not only was he a farmer, he was also steeped in the culture of the Welsh countryside and became a highly-respected author. He would take two or three of us in his car to various farms, to Dyffryn in Lampeter, to Ty'n Llofft in Silian, to Nant-y-Benglog in Capel Seion, to Troed-yr-Aur, Brongest, and to the different marts to see the shorthorns and other breeds. Occasionally, in the mart, he would buy a cow. I was with him once when he bought from Roscoe Lloyd a cow called Primrose. Roscoe Lloyd's sons – one in particular – would later play an important part in my life.

The whole point of visiting these different localities was to view the various creatures and to learn something from those visits. Richard Phillips would instruct us what qualities to look for in the different breeds. Then we could decide amongst ourselves which of the creatures had merits, and which had inferior qualities. And then we would return to Argoed to discuss our experiences.

The annual YFC Rally was held on the first Saturday of June. And that is still the case There were three very important Saturdays, all within three weeks of each other. The date of the Rally would be the middle one. On the previous Saturday the annual meeting of the Sunday School classes was held at Tabor Chapel. And on the Saturday following the Rally we would hold our annual YFC outing.

In terms of dates, they were the most important trinity in the local calendar.

There were other important dates in the farming calendar. Every farm would have its own date for shearing and for threshing. And we would all help out within a kind of exchange system. Because I was in charge of the sheep, Uncle Morgan would send me to the surrounding farms when their shearing days came around. Then, on our shearing day, people from those other farms would help us. There was no payment in cash involved – only an exchange of labour, of manpower.

It was a proud day for me when I had my first pair of shears. I took them to William Evans Tanglogau to be sharpened. He was the local expert. Most shearers sharpened their own pairs of shears. But at weekends they would go to the expert for a proper sharpening.

I was busily shearing one day when D.C. Morgan, the butcher called on his round. He offered to show me how shearing should really be done. He borrowed my shears but he accidentally cut the sheep more than once.

'Mr Morgan,' I said, 'you shouldn't cause so many cuts.'

'I know,' he answered. 'But as a butcher I tend to get between the skin and the meat. You have to get between the fleece and the skin.'

On shearing days I would exchange with Penglanowen, Tanglogau, Pantybarwn, Pengelli and Brynchwith. In those days it was the fashion to drive the sheep up to the mountains for the summer months. It's different now. These days the mountain people send their sheep down from the mountains over the winter. Tanglogau, for years, would send their sheep to Bryneithinog, Pontrhydfendigaid where brothers Dai and Joe Morgan farmed. And on the first Saturday in July I would go there for the shearing.

God's people: Olwen's parents, John in my arms
and Olwen at my side.

Four generations of Jones: John, Mam, Celine and me.

Winning the David Lloyd Memorial Cup at Eisteddfod Môn in 1970.
On my left is David Lloyd's brother, William.

The Question Master in full flight on *Siôn a Sian*, 1973.

The Singer on song!

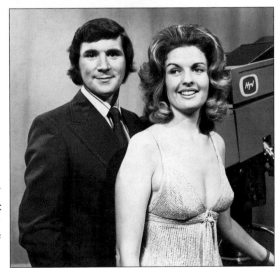

The glint and the glamour of *Siôn a Siân*: with Jenny Ogwen, the perfect hostess!

Llanilar YFC, 1979.

The Four Wise Men: casting a shrewd eye over the shire horses in the company of William Caerberllan, Gwilym Tremaelgoch and Wil Llys.

One of my three great heroes, Richard Rees, Pennal.

With the second of my great heroes, Alan Jones.

The Great and the Good: filming *Cefn Gwlad*
with Lord Geraint of Ponterwyd.

Cefn Gwlad again celebrating one of the great characters, Jac Arthur.

One horse, two men and two dogs in the snow! This programme, featuring Dan Garreg Ddu, won first prize at the Celtic Film Festival.

Two particularly powerful ponies struggle to carry Shoni Ystradfellte and me!

Celebrating St David's Day with Hywel Gwynfryn.

I would be so excited by the prospect that I couldn't sleep a wink the night before. In the morning, so that I looked like a proper shearer, I would wrap my bib-and-brace around my shears. On the way, with Evans Tanglogau, Evan Williams Rhandir Uchaf and Huw Pantybarwn, we would stop at the shop in Lledrod. There, emulating the others, I would buy a packet of twenty Players and a box of Swan matches. And with those in my pocket I would, at last, be a real shearer.

It was great at Bryneithinog. The barn would be packed with shearers, those who sheared sheep on one side and those shearing lambs on the other. My chore during the early years was to distribute the strips of cloth used to tie the sheep's feet. Ever-present would be a lame man, John Gwndwn Gwinau. He would administer pills to the sheep. Having been sheared, the sheep would be placed on a bed of reeds to be individually marked with hot pitch. And then John would administer the anti liver-fluke tablets before they were set free.

While dozens of men sheared away in the barn, the women would be hard at work preparing the dinner, which would always be followed by thick rice pudding liberally sprinkled with sultanas. It was at Bryneithinog that I first met Charles Arch. He was shearing the lambs, a task that only the very best of shearers were allowed to undertake. Charles and I have remained the best of friends ever since.

I would return home in the late evening with Moc Tanglogau. He would transport the male lambs in a trailer so that they could be fattened on lusher pastures. Moc would be driving his old Major TVO tractor which, in those days, did not boast the luxury of a cab.

As on shearing days, there would be an exchange of

labour on threshing days as well. We had two threshing days during the year. In the autumn we would produce ground corn for the cattle, enough to last the winter. Then, in spring, we would thresh in order to produce seedcorn. And that, of course, would be stored in the loft above the storehouse.

The task of a junior farmhand, or someone like me who was still a novice, was to carry the waste chaff that was spewed out from under the threshing machine. When it was oat chaff, that would be added to the store of chaff already in the barn. But barley chaff was useless and would be taken out to the field in a heap and burnt. It would smoulder there for days. But it was a bitch of a job.

I remember having to cope with it at Argoed. That night there was to be an eisteddfod held in the village. The chaff and all the dust had affected my eyes badly. And to irritate them even more, I had been continually rubbing them. By the end of the day I looked like a rabbit suffering from myxomatosis. Despite swilling my eyes time and time again the swelling remained. But it needed more than swollen eyes to keep me away from the eisteddfod.

The thresher who would visit the area with his machine was Huw Williams, Maesgwyn. His son, Hywel, was also an agricultural contractor. Huw would arrive after dark, towing the huge machine behind his Massey Harris tractor. And by torch-light he would set up the threshing machine ready for the morning.

Often in the autumn we would thresh corn ricks. Uncle was an expert at building ricks. I would toss the sheaves to him and he would expect them to land by his side every time. He would stand on one side of the rick and I would have to make sure that the sheaf landed on his inside, within easy reach of his right hand. And he expected every sheaf to land with its end facing forwards and the top facing backwards. Should even one land back to front I could expect a light box on the ears at the end of the day. There would be no need to ask what had earned that rebuke. I would know.

Llangwrddon was a closely-knit community. We very seldom had strangers settling down in the area. But the Thomases from Abercegir, to the north of Machynlleth, settled in Penglanowen Fawr. Naturally, as people from the north, they would be known to us as Gogs; *gogledd* meaning 'north' in Welsh. Fred and Beryl, who had strong northern accents, began their married life there. The North Wales accent was rather strange to our ears. Once, as I came home from threshing at Brynchwith, I saw Fred phoning from the kiosk. Very few homes had telephones then. And I still remember the kiosk's telephone number, it was Llanilar 207.

Living near Fred and Beryl were the three brothers Glyn, Tom and John, all of them bachelors at the time. You could never have wished for better neighbours, even in Heaven. On this particular evening, Tom was out on the road and he told me that Fred was phoning the maternity ward to find out whether his wife had given birth. And as Fred came out, Tom shouted across the road to ask if there was any news. Fred shouted back that everything was fine. Beryl's baby had arrived. The word he used for baby in his dialect was *cog*: and I hadn't understood, so I asked Tom what Fred had said. 'Damn,' said Tom, 'I think he said his wife had given birth to a Gog.' He, like me, had misunderstood the Montgomeryshire accent in which *cog* means a child. Gog, on the other hand, is short for *Gogleddwr,* or Northwalian.

We would exchange labour in all sorts of activities. And as we owned Troed-y-Foel in Trefenter we would often exchange with the upland farmers of Mynydd Bach. Amongst them was the brightest of them all, Dafydd Morris Jones, or Dai Morris. He was an expert trapper and was widely known as 'Dai Trapwr'. He had worked as a miner in the South Wales valleys, and knew his Bible from cover to cover. It was said that when he was trapping on the Tregaron mountain he would often engage in theological arguments with some of the visiting preachers, among them giants like Dr Martin Lloyd Jones. And as often as not Dai, would see the preacher off – having floored him with his extraordinary knowledge.

His sayings became legend in the area: he was a genuine eccentric. The mountain sheep would he herded and driven down to the Felin to be dipped. It meant a long journey along a narrow road and, one year, two of Dai's lambs suffocated in the crush while waiting to be dipped. Luckily Mrs Oliver, the blacksmith's wife, witnessed the accident and she sent for one of the Rowlands family. He quickly bled and skinned them on the spot ensuring that their deaths would not be a complete waste. Though having lost the two lambs, the message wasn't lost on Dai. He constructed his own dipping pond at Pantamlwg, the best in the neighbourhood. And it was there, from then on, that we would always dip the sheep.

Dai was always to be seen in breeches and leggings. And he would regularly walk to catch the bus. The bus only ran once a week, on a Monday, from Trefenter. That meant that on any other day he would have to walk all the way to Llangwrddon to catch it. One day there was a funeral in Llangwrddon and Dai Morris, in company with Dai Jones, a deacon and precentor, were walking down together. As they walked along a public footpath on Rhosgoch land there was a sprinkling of snow covering the fields. And both of them agreed that they would walk home together as well.

At the funeral they became separated, Dai Jones going forward to the front of the church as precentor and Dai Morris staying outside with the throng. After the funeral Dai Morris waited and waited for his friend. But seeing no sign of him he walked home through the snow on his own. Next Monday morning they met near Bethel to await the bus.

'Damn it all,' said Dai Morris, 'where did you get to after the funeral? I waited for you.'

'Sorry,' Dai Jones apologized, 'I had meant to join you but I got a lift in the car with Wmffre Pantlleinau.'

'Typical,' said Dai Morris, 'you're just like a tinker's bantam cockerel. You'll sit on anyone's bloody axle.'

Though it was a rather remote area, we had many visitors who called regularly: traders in their vans or lorries, for instance, who would call offering this and that. One of these was a fruiterer who sold apples by the box. His name was Eggerton and he came from the other side of Rhayader near the Hereford border. His sister would accompany him, a Miss Eggerton who looked like a Romany – with rings on her fingers and others dangling from her ears, a knotted scarf on her head and always dressed in silks and fishnet stockings. She would always tease me by pretending she fancied me. This made me feel rather embarrassed.

At Christmas time they would sell mistletoe as well. And at times like these she would always try to catch me under the mistletoe. Her brother urged me on one day, telling me that I should give her a Christmas kiss.

'Why don't you kiss her under the mistletoe?' he asked me.

I had very little English in those days. But I managed an answer. 'Under the mistletoe? I wouldn't kiss her under anaesthetic.'

And that reminds me of an Englishwoman who came to live in the area, one who knew very little of the ways of country folk. One day she was watching a man from Lledrod we called Jim *Sbaddwr*, which literally means Jim the Castrator, hard at work. Not realizing the significance of his nickname she thought he was called Jim Sparrow. There was Jim, busily castrating some bullocks when she asked him what they would feel like the following morning?

'Same as me on a Sunday morning,' answered Jim, 'with a bad head and an empty purse.'

Spring was one of the busiest seasons of the year. This, of course, was the lambing season. We would have brought the sheep down from Troed-y-Foel to Ty'n Cefen just before Christmas. Those that had not done so well would have been brought down even earlier. And, while they were lambing we would keep them down until early April.

The farmer was very much more on call during the spring. To me it was the most exciting time of the year. This was the time for sowing oats and barley. We always aimed at having the oats in the ground by early April and the barley seeds by early May.

Then there was the hedging. This was a specialist craft that I had to learn. I can't pretend to have been one of the best hedgers around. I never mastered the technique used by the hedgers of Breconshire, for instance. I started hedging under the eagle eye of Uncle Morgan. Once, as he was watching me at work, he told me that I wasn't driving the hedge-poles deep enough. 'If you don't drive them deeper,' he said, 'the neighbours will think that we've had a telephone installed.'

We would buy our machinery, the little that we had, from J.W. Davies, Lampeter. The salesman was a Mr Harris, a large man who was always well-dressed and who smoked a pipe. Uncle once bought a side-rake from him and it arrived as I was fencing. I was keen to have a look at this new machine so I called to Uncle and asked him whether I had driven the fence-post deep enough so that I could go over to have a look. His answer was, 'You drive that post down, my boy, until I tell you to stop.' I drove that post so deep that it disappeared into the ground.

Uncle Morgan was a fine tutor. When pitching hay, for example, he would plunge the twin-prongs of the hay-fork deep into the haycock. Then, with a strange technique he would lift that haycock by pressing the handle towards the ground and hooking one leg around the handle at the same time. Not only could he then lift the whole haycock in one movement but also the turf beneath it. I would often attempt the same technique. But I never succeeded. Yet he would never criticize me for my failure in this. He would rather encourage me.

'Now then, boy. Give it a little bit more. Swing that arm and let your armpit feel the wind.' That would always be his advice. Yes, whenever I did my best he would encourage, not criticize.

One widespread custom at the time was to spread basic slag or guano on the land. The stuff was grey and messy and arrived in bags from Port Talbot. Luckily by then we did not have to spread it by hand. We had a drill that was shared between us, Tanglogau and Penglanowen. It was a horse-drawn drill and it measured ten feet across. The gates in those days were only about eight feet wide so every time we came to a gate, the drill would have to be unhitched from the horse and manoeuvred through the opening by raising the shaft high and shuffling the wheels backwards and forwards.

I was a horseman through and through. A tractor meant nothing to me. All the furrowing would be done by horse. And Uncle Morgan was a genius when it came to working with the horses, Lion and Cholet. Lion was Cholet's son. He was quite a character. Even now I can recall those old horses and their names. Maesbeidiog kept only one horse, Star. And sometimes we would borrow Bess from Penglanowen to pair-up for potato furrowing and other tasks as well. Furrowing was no easy task. Planting potatoes was even more difficult. It meant that one horse had to walk along the top of the row. But by far the worst task was to carry and spread manure. It meant carrying load after load of dung to the potato field and spreading it across three rows. In other words, every row of dungheaps equalled three rows of potatoes. And once you carted out the dung it needed to be spread immediately before the heaps would dry and bind hard. The best dung was the one that contained a good proportion of straw.

Horses played a leading role in agriculture in those days. On using a new horse, Lewis Maesbeidiog would have to lead. But Uncle was so proficient that he would hardly have to touch the guiding lines. And watching him made me yearn for the day when I could be in charge of such wonderful shire horses. And after some time, I was. At first I was not allowed to furrow. My arms were too weak. But I was allowed to harrow on grass. And even that was far more difficult than I had ever expected. I would follow immediately behind the chain-harrow. Sometimes I would miss my step and tread on the harrow. And down I would go, flat on my back. I soon learnt to walk beside the horses.

Uncle Morgan trained shire horses in the same way as others would train dogs today. He would talk to them in a language that only he and the horses understood. 'She-back', he would murmur. 'Come-ye-'ere', and so on. But when he barked out, 'Take hold of it, horse!', you would see the old horse's neck bending like a bow and the hind legs digging deep. One of the horses he trained I remember well. He was a blue stallion and his name was Captain.

Uncle needed to remove a large standing stone that was utilized as a gatepost in Cae Ffrwd Fach at Troed-y-Foel. The gate only measured four feet across and was, of course, far too narrow. It meant physical work, a pick-and-shovel job. The days of the JCB were far in the future then. But the first task was to remove the stone gate-post. The hooks still remained in it so it could be used again for hanging the new gate. We could have bought a new wooden post, of course. But that didn't enter anyone's mind.

Having excavated around the stone, Uncle hitched old Captain to it. I can see him now, Captain's hind legs holding firm like the legs of the anchor man in a tug-o'-war team. And Uncle growling low, urging him on, 'You pull it, my old horse'. And pull it he did. I can still see that stone rising out of the ground this very minute.

It was experiences such as these that made me dream and make a vow, 'Damn! One day I'll be a farmer myself. And when I am a farmer, I'll have a horse just like Captain.'

5

Revs and Reverends

For years we were without a minister at Tabor. But we did have a vicar in the parish. And he was an exceptional character. Despite the fact that Tabor chapel was my spiritual centre, the main venue for local culture and entertainment was the church, or rather the church hall and vestry. It was there that plays were performed, concerts were staged, whist drives were organized, the Young Farmers' Club members gathered.

Religion and culture was a natural mix in the neighbourhood and both chapel and church adherents were on very good terms. In the cemetery, of course, everyone would be equal. It was common ground for everybody. The land for the cemetery had been given to the parish by the Loxdale family of Castle Hill, Llanilar. And here I would like to digress: referring to the cemetery reminds me of the story involving the building of the main pillars holding the cemetery gates.

The locality was richly blessed with fine craftsmen who would do the rounds. One of these was Edwin Penbont, a carpenter and joiner. Another was Morgan Maesllyn, the blacksmith. There were two blacksmiths in the area, which meant two smithies. As well as Morgan we had Dic, or Richard Oliver. But it was Morgan who shod our horses.

Another local craftsman was Daniel Pugh Jones the

stonemason, Dai Morris Jones's father. Daniel had an accompanying journeyman, Tom Oliver. You could never imagine two personalities so unlike each other. They were the proverbial chalk and cheese. One was a staunch chapel man, a deacon at Bethel and a great humorist. Tom, on the other hand, was always on a short fuse and believed himself to be far more intelligent than Daniel.

One day they were both busily at work building a two-storey shed. The cement was raised up to the top in a bucket by means of a pulley. Initially Daniel was in charge of pulling the rope with Tom receiving the bucket at the top. Then they changed places. And Daniel, in fun, suddenly released the bucket which travelled down at a hundred miles an hour. As it smashed onto the ground, the cement shot all over Tom, who sulked and went home. Daniel didn't see him again for a week.

But as they finished building the cemetery gate pillars, Tom was able to get his revenge. With the pillars ready for the gates to be hung, they started for home on foot, a journey of three miles. They had walked two miles when Tom announced, 'Daniel, you think that you've managed to pull off quite a stroke today, haven't you?'

'Well yes, I have,' answered Daniel. 'I have pulled off quite a stroke. I've managed to finish building the two pillars. And that's more than you've ever managed in one day.'

'Perhaps you're right,' admitted Tom. 'But you don't understand, do you? You must be daft. You forgot to fit the hinges.'

Tom was right. Daniel had forgotten to insert the hinges. And by the following morning the cement would have set and it would then be too late to insert them. Tom had realized this before they had packed up work that afternoon but had decided to keep quiet about it until they were close to home. So Daniel had to walk all the way back to fit the hinges before the cement hardened.

Yes, much of the local activities revolved around the church and the chapel. And as a faithful chapel-goer in those days it is little wonder that I came to respect religious leaders. And especially the local vicar.

The vicar of the parishes of Llwngwrddon and Lledrod then was the Reverend Tawe Jones, a remarkable man. Even at that time, when ecumenism had never even been thought of, he preached at our Thanksgiving service at Tabor. That, naturally, didn't please everyone. But that's the kind of man Tawe was. He was progressive.

When whist drives or plays were to be staged as a means of raising money for good causes, it was Tawe who organized them. And under his leadership the little hall would be packed to the rafters with people, many of them locals. These events would also attract people from a wider area as well. Always amongst them would be ten or more of the Bont boys who travelled together from Pontrhydfendigaid in an old Austin 16 driven by Dick Davies. To the Bont boys he would be known as Dic Bach for the simple reason that he was so big. One night on his way to a whist drive at Llangwrddon he drove slap bang into Cefn Coch's milk stand.

Tawe was noted for his hearty laugh. And I immediately took to him. And as we didn't have a minister, Tawe was our man. He would get to his feet in the vestry behind the church, the audience having packed the building for a play, perhaps. He would peep between the curtains and seeing that the place was heaving he would announce calmly, 'There we are. Good. Nice to see so many of you turning out. Make more room for each other and we'll get by.'

76

He came with us once on the Young Farmers' Club annual outing. And it got pretty late by the time we got home. It must have been around three o' clock on Sunday morning. Some of the village gossips had heard that a few of us had been rather drunk. And they decided to ask Tawe what had happened.

'Did you go on the trip, Mr Jones?'

'Yes indeed, I did.'

'It got very late by the time you got home.'

'Well, yes. We travelled a fair distance.'

'Did you stop for . . . food or anything like that?'

'Yes, we had food.'

'Were some of the lads drunk?'

'The boys had a very pleasurable time. The best trip ever. Yes indeed. And I'll be going with them next year again.'

And off went Tawe, with no one any the wiser.

He was a great benefactor. He gave some of us driving lessons. It was Tawe who taught Dafydd Evans, Cnwc y Barcut to drive. But things got a bit hairy when Dai Ty'n Rhyd bought a motorbike. Dai was an apprentice with a firm of builders, Davies Aberarth, and he would ride home for the various rehearsals in preparation for the YFC Rally. One night he arrived in the village and asked, 'Is Ty'n Cefen here?'

And I should explain here one of the strange traits of rural life. No one would ask for Dai Jones or Dai Jenkins, not even for Dai Ty'n Cefen or Dai Ty'n Rhyd. They would ask, rather, 'Is Ty'n Cefen here? Is Ty'n Rhyd here? Llaindelyn? Brynchwith? Ty'n Llwyn?' We would be known not by our names or even by our nicknames but rather by the names of our homes.

Anyway, Dai had arrived looking for me. And he was

told that I hadn't arrived. Off he rode to meet me. But on the Tanrallt bend he rode straight in to Tawe's car. The vicar drove an old Ford which had a running board alongside it. Tawe got out of the car.

'Are you all right?'

Dai, in fact, had suffered quite a bad injury. If I remember correctly, he broke a bone in his foot.

'There we are,' said Tawe. 'Remember to take care on these bad bends. Try telling yourself that there is a woman driving to meet you on every bend.'

Then he laughed heartily, as if suggesting that women should never be allowed to drive. Political correctness had not been invented then. Yes, Tawe Jones. I would place him very high on the list of local characters. And he lived to a grand old age, thank God.

Having mentioned Dai's motorbike this, perhaps, is the right place for me to mention my first car. I bought it from Rhys Benjamin, Brynpyllau. Rhys kept a shop where he sold virtually everything. Should you even ask for Jesus Christ's left sandal, Rhys would find it somewhere in the shop. And if he couldn't, he'd order it.

Rhys would buy cars up in Queensferry. He would drive there with three or four friends who would drive cars back for him. I bought my car from him on the never-never. Dad told Uncle to let me buy the car myself so that I would learn how to save and appreciate money. It was a grey Standard 10, and I still remember the price. It was £240, and the registration number was FF 9745. The FF would remind me of Fenella Fielding, the actress. But the FF meant something completely different to some of my friends. I will not elaborate here!

My experienced driver was Tom Ty'n Llan from the Red

Dragon School of Motoring in Aberystwyth. And I passed my test the very first time in Machynlleth, where I drove the tester's car, a Triumph Herald. And this time, no, I don't remember the number.

The price of petrol wasn't disproportionately high in those days. But without a rise in my earnings it was quite difficult. So I found a way of making money on the side. I would buy 174lb linen sacks that had held animal food-stuffs for nine pence each. Ifor Lloyd would then buy them from me. What he did with them afterwards, I still have no idea. The important thing was that there was a profit of three pence on every sack. Sometimes the boot of my car would be full of sacks, around two hundred of them. And it was through this arrangement that Ifor and I became firm friends. Later he would be best man at my wedding.

I would also sometimes make the occasional ten bob through helping Dai Tanybryn to catch rabbits. He would sell them to Simpkins, a butcher in Aberystwyth. This, of course, was before the myxomatosis plague decimated the rabbit population.

One important advantage of having my own car was being able to travel further to do my courting. The car may not have had reclining seats. But it did have a back seat. On every Good Friday an eisteddfod was held at Llanilar and also at Llanddewi Brefi, some ten miles further south. I had just found myself a new girlfriend, and now I decided to clean the car in order to please her. I had bought a special perfume, a kind of Air Wick for the inside, which I would refer to as a fragrant stink. And I bought some special polish for the body to give it a fine sheen. But I must have misread the instructions. Starting from the bottom I smeared the polish all over the car. But by the time I reached the roof, the wax had dried. I had thought in terms of boot polish, believing that the longer it dried, the better it would shine. But in this case I failed miserably, and I was forced to attend the two eisteddfodau in a two-tone car that, from halfway down, shone like a silver shilling, but from half-way up was a dullish white.

But I digress again. To return to vicars and ministers – and strangely enough, there is a strong connection in this case between a car and a minister. As I have explained, we did not have a minister when I was a boy. Neither had there been one during the previous generation. I think the last one to have ministered at Tabor was a Mr Edwards who lived in the Commercial.

Then, at last, a minister arrived. He was an Anglesey man, R.E. Hughes, or Ted Hughes who came to live at Bryngolau, Penuwch. He had worked as a farmhand but had left the land to go to college where he graduated and qualified as a minister. He was inducted as minister serving Blaenplwyf, Tabor and Elim. He did not drive so we, the young men of Llangwrddon, decided to teach him. He bought a Morris 1000, light blue in colour and its number was XAC something-or-other. I would call round to visit him on Saturday nights and take him out for driving lessons. We had great fun.

Once, when he was preaching in Llanrwst, he had found his own way up the previous Thursday but had asked some of us, Dai Cnwc, Ieu and myself to drive up to Seion Chapel, Llanrwst to pick him up. Leaving on Sunday afternoon we weren't very sure of our bearings. But we made it to Llanrwst in good time. We found a chapel but we weren't sure whether it was Seion. So we crept quietly into the lobby and listened to the preacher. We recognized his voice immediately. It was easy for us to detect the Anglesey accent.

We picked Ted up and drove him first of all to his home in Rhoscefnhir near Pentraeth. The name of his home was Yr Orsedd, and he was known locally as *Ted yr Orsedd*. His father was the local blacksmith, and he was well-known in horse circles as a man who had shod some notable horses in preparation for many of the top shows.

Then, after supper in Anglesey, we started back and reached Llangwrddon around half-past-three on Monday morning. It felt as if we had been to the ends of the earth.

R.E. fitted in perfectly in our community and he managed to turn us into faithful members of the chapel. Not that we needed much persuasion. We already were faithful adherents. The chapel, even without a minister was, after all, a natural meeting place for us.

R.E. would compère the *Cwrdd Bach*. He had a store of jokes and he made the audience laugh. They were harmless jokes that he had heard, no doubt, when he had been a theological student. What made them funnier was his strange dialect. He stayed in the locality for a good many years and he certainly made his mark. And not only at Tabor. He also became a staunch supporter of the Young Farmers' Club.

As part of the chapel activities a bi-monthly meeting was held where representatives of the various chapels in the area would present an address. And of course, my turn came round. I will always remember the subject. It was, 'Persevere with Reading'. The late Reverend John David Jones, Blaenplwyf, wrote it for me. It must have been about fifty pages long. And for a while I thought that I really would end up being a preacher.

J.D. Jones was a fine man who was in his element when he was out hunting and fishing. He was my wife's uncle. And when I first met him we joked about the fact that he was John David Jones and I was David John Jones. I told him that he must have been born back to front.

Visiting preachers would often call at Ty'n Cefen, especially in the summer when many of those that had left to become ministers came back to the old neighbourhood. One of them was Rhys Cefn Coch, or Rhys Griffiths who had been made a lecturer at Caerleon. Rhys had a sister who was quite a personality. Her real name must have been Louisa. But she was known to everyone as Lowsa. I was with her once when one of her cows was calving. There were complications as it was a breech birth. And some of the neighbours went over to help ease the delivery by turning the calf and pulling. The Penglanowen boys were there, so were Moc and Wil Tanglogau and Eben Maesbeidiog. They've all gone now. And I, although just a lad, was with them. William Evans Tanglogau was in charge. He was responsible for ensuring that the calf's head faced the right way.

Everything turned out successfully and we all breathed a sigh of relief when Lowsa asked, 'Where in the world am I going to put it?'

And Wil Tanglogau answered, 'You put it wherever you like, Lowsa. But don't ask me to put it back in.'

Tom Williams Rhosgoch would sometimes help her. And Tom, if anything went wrong, would have his own personal exclamation. He wouldn't swear. He wouldn't even say 'Heavens above!' or 'My God!' Tom would say, *yr hollamwriaid mawr*! What it meant, I had no idea. Neither had Tom. But it sounded impressive.

Tom had been a talented singer and gave me a few lessons. If he happened to call round, Aunty Hannah would often call me in from my work to sing to Tom. But how in the world could I sing for Tom Williams after coming straight in from cleaning out the hen-house?

Tom would gather the hay for Lowsa. She didn't own a tractor but she did have a shire horse, or rather a mare. Her name was Lock and she was always to be seen on the farmyard. Tom would dress her and put her between the shafts of the rake. Sometimes Tom would dress up as well by wearing a bowler hat. And on a cold day he would also wear a long black coat and gloves. When Evan Williams once saw him in that rig-out he exclaimed, 'Good God! Who's that raking the hay for Lowsa? Lord Kenyon?'

One day when I called, Tom and Lock were busy in the field and Lowsa asked me to take him some tea and cake. She cut a chunk of cake and spread some jam on two slices of bread-and-butter. But she had a problem with the tea. She didn't own a Thermos flask so she grabbed a jug from off the dresser and emptied it of its contents of needles, cotton reels and buttons of all colours and sizes. And without even bothering to swill it out she poured the boiling-hot tea straight into the jug.

I took everything out to the field in a basket and handed it over to Tom. Lowsa hadn't thought of including a cup so Tom drank the tea straight from the jug. Having eaten all the bread and jam he tackled the cake. And then he gulped down what was left of the tea. And there I stood, waiting patiently for the jug in case it broke. It was a valuable jug, probably handed down from generation to generation. As he swallowed the last drop, Tom choked. I thought he was about to kick the bucket. Then he gagged and coughed and with his eyes bulging like organ-stops and his face a bright red he brought up half the cake and a button as large as a gob-stopper. The button must have stuck to the bottom of the jug and had been worked loose by the hot tea.

Eventually, having got his breath back, he handed me the jug – and then the button. 'Take this back to Lowsa, my boy,' he said. 'And tell her that I nearly choked on a button from a pair of long johns from her jug.'

Lowsa's brother, Rhys, was one of a number of ministers that would call at Ty'n Cefen. Another was John Davies, Y Gopa, Pontarddulais who used to live at Mynydd Mawr. I was one of many children who heard him preach of a Sunday evening. He would sometimes take off his coat and become so passionate that steam would rise and sweat would run down his cheeks. John Davies did not address God as someone who was far away. He would address Him personally. Many a time I turned to gaze at the gallery, so convinced was I that God was really up there staring down at John Davies.

One regular visitor was Walter Morgan from Tregaron. He would arrive on a Saturday night, catching the bus to Rhyd-yr-Efail and then walking to Tabor where he would spend the night at the Chapel House. He loved that walk. He wasn't a minister. He was, rather, a lay preacher who was a tailor by trade.

Walter would always sport a dickey-bow. And in features he looked exactly like an old portrait of William Williams Pantycelyn that I had seen in a book. And I believe that he was aware of the resemblance as he would often bring Williams into his sermons. He was an excellent preacher.

On his way to Tabor he would call with us. If Walter was preaching on a Sunday I could guarantee that he would call.

He would then stop for supper before continuing on his journey. It's quite possible that he ate another meal there as well. I can't be certain. But that sort of thing was common in those days. To be a preacher you needed a strong stomach.

Walter would only eat free-range eggs. And he would usually have two. And over supper he would relate all sorts of tales. He once told us of an epitaph he had seen on a gravestone in Trefeurig churchyard. I never saw the stone but I never forgot the epitaph even though I only heard it the once.

> *For ye who come my grave to see,*
> *Prepare yourself to follow me;*
> *For here I lie in this cold clay*
> *Until the resurrection day.*

Being a tailor, I suppose it was to be expected that his appearance should be different from that of other people. He would wear a black coat, pin-striped trousers and he always carried a walking stick. And his walk was always graceful. People like Walter are sorely missed. They would grace the neighbourhood with their presence. And the sadness of the situation is that it all seems as if it was only yesterday. I don't consider myself as old. After all, I'm only slightly over sixty. And I remember them well.

There was Victor Thomas from Borth. Like J.D. Jones, of Aberdwr, Tregaron, he came originally from the vicinity of Bont and Tregaron. It's strange how so many of them came from that same area.

Another minister that comes to mind is William Jones who came to Bronnant. He had come to the area from

Bangor. But I know for a fact that he had never seen in Bangor the strange sight that he witnessed one day in Bronnant.

He would call regularly in one particular home for a cup of tea and a chat. One day the occupant took him out to show him the garden and to show him, in particular, his new outside toilet. And that's when William Jones saw his first-ever Elsan closet which had a chimney jutting out of the roof.

'Well, what a strange little closet,' said William Jones. 'What's the purpose of the chimney?'

'Damn it all,' said the old man, 'that's where the farts go.'

Men of the Cloth meant a great deal to me. And thanks to the Young Farmers' Club we would invite some of the big guns, or the 'Eight-inch Nails', as we would call them, to address us. Among them was Idwal Jones, Llanrwst. And also John Roberts, Caernarfon. And I remember Gwilym Tilsley preaching at Tabor. His voice still reverberates in my ears to this day.

Incidentally, one Cardiganshire minister was rebuked by one of the elders for not being fiery enough in his preaching. 'You need to be like one of the old Eight-inch Nails,' said the elder. 'True,' admitted the minister, 'but what use is an eight-inch nail in a plank that is only an inch thick?'

Yes, I was raised in a household that respected religion. As far as the farm went, there were strict rules I had to adhere to, especially on a Sunday. For instance, I was not allowed to whistle while I worked. Yes, I suppose that Uncle and Aunty were a little strict in that respect. And of course, I would be expected to attend chapel.

The golden rule, however, was that only tasks that were totally necessary could be undertaken on a Sunday. For one thing I wasn't allowed to do any pulping. Everything had to be prepared on the previous day. So, on a Saturday evening I would place the pulp on top of the chaff so that the sap from the mangolds would have dried by the next morning. I would place the mixture in sacks, which meant a great deal of kneeling. And what with treacle being an integral ingredient of the mixture my trouser-legs would harden like plastic.

I read very little in those early days, the reason being that there was very little reading matter in the house. We received the two local papers, *The Welsh Gazette* and the *Cambrian News*. The *Welsh Farm News* also arrived regularly. Sometimes we would borrow a copy of the *Western Mail* from Lewis Maesbeidiog. And the only reason Uncle had for borrowing that was to read through the births, marriages and deaths column. It was only later that we started taking *The People*. And that would not be read till Monday morning.

Sometimes I would complain to Uncle about the lack of reading matter. His answer would be, 'Read your Bible, my boy. That will do you more good than reading anything else.'

And perhaps he was right. He usually was.

6

Hear my Song

As a singer, I didn't start competing seriously until I was in my early twenties, moving out to local eisteddfodau within a radius of about 15 miles. What made this possible was buying a car. This allowed me to move out of my immediate locality. And this, in turn, prompted me to compete far more regularly.

My first vocal tutor was Professor Redvers Llewellyn from the Music Department at the University in Aberystywth. He had been to Covent Garden and was Sir Thomas Beecham's principal soloist. Whenever Sir Thomas needed a baritone for a concert or for a recording he would give Redvers a call.

Redvers came from Briton Ferry near Neath and was a very witty character. He boasted a pucker English accent and would always refer to me as 'David'.

Elocution meant very little to Redvers. In the National Eisteddfod held at Aberafan in 1966, where two Cardis shone, Dic Jones winning the Chair and Dafydd Jones, Ffair Rhos, the Crown, I qualified for the stage in the under-25 solo. I had to present two works, *Plygeingan* (Morning Song) by Idris Lewis and that very difficult piece, Puccini's *Nessum Dorma*, was the other. In that second piece there is a high B Flat, which is very awkward. The relevant sentence goes, *Na, neb nes im' ei sibrwd ar dy fin.* (No, no-one lest I whisper it on your lip.) And it was the word *sibrwd* that made it difficult. Redvers's suggestion was, 'David, to hell with the "sibrwd". Say "sebroid" instead.' To Redvers, the meaning was secondary.

My first elocution tutor was Ifan Maldwyn of Machynlleth. I would visit him often on Saturday nights with Erfyl Llaindelyn. There, in his home in Heol y Doll near the station, Ifan would teach us. He was full of fanciful inventions. He could visualize a song by turning the words into pictures. He was the best. I could always tell if a particular singer was being trained by Ifan Maldwyn. The words of the song would always be easily understood. That was his trade-mark. Before tackling the song he would always ask me to recite the words so that their meaning would become clear in my mind.

It was Ifan who taught me all the leading solos. Unfortunately he was already quite elderly by the time he taught me. He had retired from his job as a guard with British Rail. But he kept himself extremely busy. As well as teaching soloists like me, he also conducted the local choir and a local band.

I gradually spread my wings competitively by singing in eisteddfodau throughout Ceredigion. And at that time the county could boast an eisteddfod in almost every village or parish, especially so in the west and north. By now I was a fairly competent competitor.

The first eisteddfod of note for me was at Tyngraig near Ystrad Meurig. The adjudicator was Idris Daniel who, in his day, was one of Wales's foremost singers. And it was there that I was fortunate enough to win my very first cup. And it was Idris who urged me to persevere.

Three of us would usually travel together, Erfyl, Dai Ty'n

Llwyn and myself. The Ty'n Llwyn family was well-known in eisteddfodic circles, and over the years I depended on them for transport. When I was a schoolboy it was Mrs. Jones, Dai's mother, who would take us all to the various festivals and concerts. I can remember them buying a black Austin Somerset. Its registration number was CEJ 828. Then they bought a blue Austin Cambridge, MEJ 314. That was some car, and I recall telling William Jones, 'Damn, this is quite a car you've got.'

'Yes,' he said, 'it's a wonderful car.'

'It looks to me as if it could shift a bit. This one will pass everything.'

'Yes,' said William, 'everything except for a petrol pump.'

What with the Young Farmers' Club activities – and courting – competing was still not exactly top on my list of priorities. I would follow the various agricultural shows and other country activities diligently. But the competing bug gradually took over.

Erfyl and Dai dropped out. Erfyl's period in college came to an end and he left to work in England. And Dai confined himself to local events. And this is when I really began travelling far and wide to compete throughout the north and the south. And I began to taste success on a regular basis. And gradually, with more prizes under my belt and more prize-money in my pocket I came to the attention of Alun Williams from the BBC. He was organizing auditions in Aberystwyth for talents who would take part in an inter-county competition. Three times I was chosen to represent Ceredigion. And this was a real boost for my career. And it also brought in much-needed extra earnings. Looking back, I think the BBC paid better in those days than it does now. At least, it seemed to be so.

Ceredigion would invariably reach the final round. The soloists who represented some of the other counties included many that I would compete against on the eisteddfod circuit. There was Tom Davies, Bryniog representing Denbighshire, a wonderful oratorio singer; Margaret Williams would represent Anglesey; the late Alun Watkins would compete for Caernarfonshire; Margaret Mynydd Mawr would sing for Carmarthenshire. She went on to be a professional singer. Members of the O'Neill family from Pontarddulais also competed regularly.

The final round, with four counties taking part, would be televised. And that led to my first appearance on the small screen. It was quite an experience. It meant almost a week's preparation for my visit to Cardiff. I took a bath on Wednesday night. I shone my shoes on Thursday night. On Friday night I packed everything in readiness. And then off I went before dawn broke on Saturday morning.

In the meantime, as the singing gradually took over more and more of my life, I got married. At any wedding, etiquette is very important. And fortunately I had attended a course on the very subject as part of the Young Farmers' Clubs programme. That course came appropriately enough just before I attended my first wedding reception. The wedding reception of Moc Tanglogau and Elsie Cwm Gwenyn, Llangeitho was held at the Central Hotel, Aberystwyth. A few days previously I had attended the etiquette course at the Marine Hotel, also at Aberystwyth. There we were instructed as to what items of cutlery to use, when and in what order.

Following a lecture we were asked to demonstrate what we had learnt. And we were all to be awarded marks at the end. Every time we realized that we had a spare knife or fork we would hide the evidence by pocketing the surplus item. As we left for home, the cutlery rattling in our pockets, you could have sworn that there was a percussion band playing at the Marine.

Olwen and I were married on October 22nd, 1966, the day after the terrible disaster at Aberfan. And I well remember the Revd R.E. Hughes asking, in his prayer, for God to comfort all those bereaved families. And there I was, whispering to Ifor Lloyd, my best man, and asking him what had happened at Aberfan? One of the worst tragedies in the history of the world had occurred only 100 miles away, and I had been too busy running around to have even heard of the disaster.

But life had to go on, and Olwen and I left for our honeymoon in Scotland. By now I was a farmer in my own right. Olwen and I had bought our own herd and were milk producers. I rang home one night to hear that one of the cows, old Duchess, had died through over-feasting in the rape field. And there and then the honeymoon was abandoned. We were home by Thursday morning in case any more cows were suffering.

Gradually Olwen and I, with the backing of my parents-in-law, began diversifying. At our newly-built bungalow on our own land we started putting up visitors. From the very beginning we attracted visitors from all parts of Britain, especially from the English Midlands. The Birmingham Fortnight, that traditional holiday period for Midlanders, would bring them by the dozen.

At that time we were practically self-sufficient. We would slaughter our own animals and use our own vegetables. It was an ideal way of making a little bit extra, a bonus on top of what we made from farming. And we began making a living wage.

With Olwen being kept so busy, she seldom managed to accompany me on my various journeys around Wales on the eisteddfod circuit. But at weekends her father would keep me company. He was one of the Penbryn boys from Bronnant. He was the tenth of 16 children and as such he had been baptized Decimus, or to give him his full name, John Decimus Davies. This Latinized naming was a family tradition. He had brothers who had been named Quintus, Decimus, Tredecimus, Octavius and so on.

I would be competing somewhere or other every Saturday night and I continued visiting Ifan Maldwyn every Thursday night. One or two adjudicators had advised me to seek more tuition, more discipline. One of those was Gwilym Gwalchmai who was a music tutor at the Manchester Royal College of Music. He called me to one side one night and asked me whether I had ever considered attending the Royal? I jumped at the chance and immediately applied for a grant which would enable me to attend college by commuting regularly between Llanilar and Manchester. But unfortunately I was told that I would have to attend full-time.

This prompted Gwilym Gwalchmai to suggest am alternative. He arranged for me to visit Colin Jones, a voice tutor at Manchester who lived at Rhosllanerchrugog. At that time he conducted the prestigious Rhos Male Voice Choir. Today he has his own choir, The Colin Jones Singers.

I was due to start with Colin on a Sunday. But exactly a week before I should have started, Gwilym Gwalchmai died suddenly. He had just arrived home from attending chapel at Llangadfan. I attended his funeral on the following Friday at Llanerfyl where I met Colin Jones. He told me that he was happy to comply with Gwilym Gwalchmai's request but suggested postponing the first visit for a week.

On my way up to Rhos for that very first lesson I was driving through Llanidloes. I stopped there to buy a local newspaper, *The County Times*, and there on the front page was a photograph of Gwilym Gwalchmai and his obituary. It was a strange and rather frightening coincidence. There I was reading the funeral report of the man who was responsible for my journey.

For six months with Colin I did not compete. Indeed, I did not make one public appearance on stage. It was the following spring when I started competing again when I won at the champion solo at the Minsterly eisteddfod from among 30 competitors. Then I competed in the larger festivals. At the Pantyfedwen Festival at Pontrhydfendigaid I won the male solo award. At the Cardigan Festival I won first prize in the solo for the under 30's. And as one half of a duet, I returned home from Cardigan with £135 in my pocket, a huge sum at that time for a simple farmer from rural Ceredigion.

I competed twice in the Urdd Festival, the youth equivalent of the National Eisteddfod and twice won the tenor solo competition, at Carmarthen and Llanrwst. It was a great boost to have won both in the north and the south.

Then came 1970, the Golden Year. I had only intended competing in a few festivals. I decided to concentrate instead on preparing myself thoroughly. I won again at Minsterly and at Cardigan. At the Anglesey Festival at Llanddeusant I won the David Lloyd Memorial Award. The trophy for that competition had been donated by a local woman and it was worth £100. There were 43 of us in the prelim. The donor, who was present, made it known after the prelims that she would like to see the cup go to either Margaret Lewis Jones, who had just recovered from a terrible accident when she had suffered serious burns, or to 'that lad from Llanilar'. I won first prize, Margaret came second and Howel Price of Mostyn came third. I still have that cup and I treasure it greatly.

I was privileged to compete during the Golden Age of eisteddfodau. In Ceredigion alone there were a dozen or more of us under-25 years old competing regularly, many of them soloists who made it big in both the National and other prestigious festivals. There was Angela Rogers Lewis, Carol Jones Pontrhydygroes, Ifor Lloyd, Dafydd Edwards Bethania. Then, from further afield, the O'Neill family – Dennis, Pat and Doreen. Dennis is now a world star and it's nice to remember that I did occasionally beat him. He also beat me on many occasions. That's how it was. And as for the champion solo in those days, it was as good as anything you would find professionally today.

Then there were the old stagers like Berwyn Davies Felinfach, Ifan Lloyd Crugybar and the king of them all as a vocalist, Lloyd Davies Tal-y-bont. He was an outstanding character. At a certain eisteddfod the adjudicator, Andrew Williams, decided to place Ifan Lloyd and Lloyd Tal-y-bont as equal winners of the champion solo. Then the secretary intervened, explaining to the adjudicator that there could be only one winner as the first prize was a cup.

Andrew Williams apologized and began to address the audience with his re-assessment of the situation. Before he was given the chance to announce the name of the overall winner, Lloyd Tal-y-bont interrupted him. Standing in the gallery, his voice echoing round the chapel, he bellowed, 'Give Ifan the cup, mate. I've got hundreds of them at home.'

At Capel y Groes, Lloyd was to sing *Brad Dunravon*

(The Dunravon Treachery), a dramatic piece about a pirate. Earlier in the champion solo competition his rendition of *My Hand Shall Conquer All* by Felice had made the building quake. The adjudicator was Dr Leslie Wyn Evans, one who was always dapperly dressed with every hair on his head in place. He never needed notes for his adjudication. He spoke off the cuff. That was one of his peculiarities. He first upset Lloyd by referring to him as Llwyd. He upset him even further by advising him to curb his voice. 'I could feel a certain uneasy flush on my face when he sang *forte,*' he said, referring to Lloyd's rendition of the Felice piece.

So, not having won in the champion class, Lloyd rose and strode forward to compete in the Welsh solo competition. Having reached the adjudicator's table he flung the copy of *Brad Dynrafon* in front of Doctor Leslie exactly as if he was throwing something into the rubbish bin and thundered, 'Now then, mate, if you want to remain healthy you had better stand at the back or I'll be liable to blow your head off your shoulders.'

And he sang *Brad Dynrafon* as I had never heard it sung before. And as I've never heard it sung since.

Lloyd was justly proud of his powerful voice. He was talking to Jenkins Pwllpridd, Lledrod one day. 'Well, Lloyd,' said Jenkins, 'I see from reading the *Radio Times* that you're singing on the wireless next Friday night. I've bought a new battery specially to hear you.'

'Well,' said Lloyd, his voice resonating as if rising from a deep dungeon, 'if your wireless is more than five years old you'd better not risk turning it on. Otherwise it will explode in little pieces.'

People would travel from far afield to compete. John Tegla Williams, for instance, would come all the way from

Trefnant to compete in small chapels in Trisant, Pontrhydygroes and Ysbyty Ystwyth. He would travel over two hours one way for nothing more than the joy of singing. The prizes were modest. The first prize for the winner of the solo under-25 at Trisant would be a weather-glass which would always be donated by the Bwlchcrwys family.

I would compete in every possible category, under-25, the Welsh solo, the hymn, the folk song, the champion solo and I would also partner someone in the duet. Every penny won would be useful in paying for the petrol. Ifor Lloyd and I often competed in the duet. We once came second in the Pantyfedwen Festival. And that was when that particular festival was at its height. It was staged then in a huge marquee.

The Pantyfedwen family deserve our thanks for sponsoring these big festivals at Pontrhydfendigaid, Cardigan and Lampeter and giving us, Welsh singers, the opportunity not only to compete but to win substantial prizes. And even more important was the chance given to people like us from the rural areas to be assessed by some of the foremost adjudicators in Britain, musical experts like Isobel Bailey, Peter Gelhorn, Arthur Reckless, Harvey Allen, Gordon Clinton, John Mitcheson and many others as well. It was an experience just to be able to sing at the prelims. Today there are many world-famous singers who served their apprenticeship in the Pantyfedwen festivals. Once at Pontrhydfendigaid I remember sharing the stage in the final of the male champion solo with Dennis O'Neill and Philip Ravenscroft. The adjudicators were Richard Rees, Pennal and Gerald Davies, Cardiff. Yes, a Golden Age indeed.

All this competing, all this travelling, naturally led to

making new friends. I can think of W.E. Williams, Llanbryn-mair for instance, one of the most enthusiastic competitors of all time. I knew him as Wil Ty Pella. He was better known as just W.E. Together we must have sung duets in most of Wales's eisteddfodau. If it meant going up north I would meet him at the Station Garage in Machynlleth. And should we be heading south, the meeting place would be the Oak Garage at Llanfarian.

We travelled the whole of Wales together. My car was liable to be full of rubbish. It was a skip on wheels. On the way to the Llangollen Eisteddfod once I made the point to Wil that I had cleared out the car.

'Good to see it,' he said. 'I had considered wearing my Wellington boots.'

Nowhere was too far for us: the Butlins Eisteddfod at Pwllheli on the last Saturday of the summer season, where there was a prize of £50 to be won there in the champion solo; Bwlchtocyn on New Year's Eve; and Christmas night at Blaenpennal. And mentioning Blaenpennal, it's worth recalling a humorous occasion. Fred Evans, who kept a watch-maker's shop at Aberystwyth was present. Fred was one of the Esgair Hendy family from Blaenpennal and there he sat in one of the front pews. The place was chock-a-block, and sharing the pew with him were some highly respectable local ladies. Fred, who had eaten heartily during the day, felt rather bloated. And try as he might, he couldn't hold back any longer and out came a rather embarrassing sound. Unperturbed, Fred smiled apologetically at them all saying, 'So sorry. Too much goose gravy.'

Sometimes I would take in two eisteddfodau the same Saturday night. I can remember competing under-25 at Llanbryn-mair and then travelling through Staylittle over to

Llanidloes and on through Rhayader on my way to Senny Bridge in time to compete there as well.

Two others that I would take in on the same night were Kerry near Newtown and Llanfachreth near Dolgellau. I have some fond memories of Llanfachreth in particular. And two aspects will remain forever among my recollections. One was the gnats that plagued the place. They would bite like a pack of Jack Russell terriers. The second is listening to Gwyndaf Evans, who was born locally and who had been Archdruid of Wales delivering his presidential address. There were around 15 of us waiting to compete in the champion solo. And there we sat on a grassy bank outside listening to him. I can remember the names of most of the singers now – Howel Price Mostyn, Wil Prysor, Ken Jones Saron, W.E. Llanbryn-mair, Margaret Lewis Jones Llanbryn-mair, Dai Croeslwyn, Bob Bach Henllan, Iwan Davies Prestatyn, Tom Gwanas and myself – and many more, with Gwyndaf addressing the audience. There we were on a warm, balmy night listening spellbound to him.

The first eisteddfod on the calendar, apart from the New Year events, was the Abergynolwyn Eisteddfod held on the first Saturday in February. This event was famous not only for its success in attracting a large number of competitors but also for the savoury faggots that the women prepared. I swear I could smell those faggots all the way from Corris as I drove there.

In Welsh there is a phrase *y cythraul canu,* which literally means 'the demon of the song' which implies that singing in Wales can create jealousy, enmity and malice. Whether it actually exists or not – indeed, whether it has ever existed – I cannot tell. But I can say this. If it ever did exist within our circle it was a very benign demon. Yes, we all yearned to win. But we were also quite prepared to lose. One Saturday night at Lampeter I won and Berwyn Davies was placed second. The following night I was appearing there for the Sunday concert and I was limping badly.

'What's wrong with your leg?' asked Berwyn.

'Damn it,' I said, 'a cow stepped on my foot while I was milking this evening.'

'Pity it didn't stamp on your bloody neck,' said Berwyn. And we both laughed heartily.

It was interesting to study the likes and dislikes of the various adjudicators. One, perhaps, would sit on the fence and award something to everyone. Such an adjudicator would be known to us as a National Assistance adjudicator as he would ensure that no one went home empty-handed. Others, like the late, great Meirion Williams would suggest all kinds of helpful advice. And I must admit that I received in my time no little favouritism from Meirion. Then there was Gwilym Gwalchmai again, with his beautiful voice and his great sympathy for all singers. Others could be a little discourteous.

I well remember Arthur Vaughan Williams, Llanrwst with his half-spectacles dangling above his nose. He was adjudicating at Dinas Mawddwy late one night – or rather, early one morning. It must have been about three o'clock and Arthur was yawning away. There we were, a dozen or more of us awaiting our turn. Trebor Gwanas took the stage to sing *Arthur yn Cyfodi* (Arthur Arising). Arthur Vaughan Williams awoke with a smile. 'Well, I'm afraid that Trebor won't win tonight,' he said. 'Arthur may have arisen but he wasn't fully awake.'

Gwyneth Alban Davies from Rhyl was a very astute adjudicator, as was Rhys Jones from Ffynnon-groyw. Down south they would tend to have as adjudicators those who were products of the music colleges. They would include Gerald Davies, Cardiff, Geraint Evans and many more. Gerald, in particular, had been through the opera scene and even though he was not a Welsh speaker he helped many of us. The Pontrhydfendigaid Festival deserves our deepest thanks for giving people like Gerald the chance to adjudicate. The National Eisteddfod would allow non-Welsh speakers on the panel of adjudicators but they would not be allowed to deliver the adjudication from the stage. But at Bont, Gerald and others, like Gordon Clinton, were allowed to do so.

To someone like me, who was a full-time dairy farmer, competing on a regular basis was a bind. It meant having to do the milking before leaving and returning in time for milking the following morning. Often I would return home from competing only to have to change immediately to my working clothes to milk the cows before catching up with a little sleep.

Then, having decided to visit Colin Jones on a regular basis, my Sundays were taken up completely. I would leave on Sunday morning around nine o'clock after the milking. It took two hours for me to travel from the farmyard at Berthlwyd to Rhos – it was exactly 100 miles one-way. Then, having arrived, Colin and I would sit down for a cup of tea at eleven. There followed two hours of tuition. I would have another cup of tea before leaving Colin and I would be back in Llanilar at five. Then it would be dinner and after that the evening's milking. It was a hard life. But if you are determined to learn a craft properly you have to be ready to make sacrifices.

It grieves me to see the great decline in the number of

eisteddfodau. In their heyday it was common to see around 40 competing at Pontrhydfendigaid on the male solo and the same number competing in the female section – and all of them brilliant soloists. In the under-25's competition the prelims would last for hours.

This was true of the Cardigan Festival as well, which would run for four days, from Thursday night to Sunday. The place would be jam-packed with competitors. Following the prelim for the champion solo in Cardigan once, with Trefor Anthony and Arthur Reckless adjudicating, I can remember four of us waiting to compete on the stage. There we were, Margaret Lewis Jones, Angela Rogers Lewis, Philip Ravenscroft and myself sitting in the caravan that doubled as the green room at a quarter-to-one in the morning.

The first prize was £100. But although it was a princely sum, it wasn't the money that counted in the end. It gave me just as much pleasure to win when there wasn't any prize money involved. When I won first prize in the Urdd Festival at Llanrwst, for example, the prize was a book token. It was only after arriving home that I realized that I would have to travel back to Llanrwst to exchange it for a book.

But back to 1970. Following quite a successful run, Colin Jones decided that I should now go for the big prestigious prizes. He advised me to concentrate on the Anglesey Festival, on the National and on Llangollen. And having won at Llanddeusant in Anglesey I turned my attention to Llangollen.

I entered – and won – the tenor solo having sung two pieces, Cesar Frank's composition *Panis Angelicus,* adapted into Welsh by W.S. Gwynn Williams, and a piece by Verdi. Competing at Llangollen was quite an experience. All six winners of the various solo competitions appeared in a prelim with two appearing in the final. I made it there together with a Spanish soprano.

From the stage I had to face twelve adjudicators. Then all twelve lined up on the stage while one of them delivered the verdict. Both of us finalists had to present two pieces, one of them our own choice and the other a song from our respective countries. I chose *Una Furtiva Lagrima* from one of Donizetti's operas and *Y Dieithryn* (The Stranger) by Morgan Nicholas. And I won.

Present in the pavilion was a girls' choir from Italy and after I sang the first piece in their language they broke into shouts of 'Bravo!' That must have been the greatest ovation I have ever received.

Back home the following Monday, after much publicity in the press and on radio and television, I was busily ploughing in Cae Cwm when I was interrupted by the arrival of two of the judges. There I was driving the old blue Power Major. It had no cab so the seagulls were using me for target practice. Obviously, to them there was no difference at all between the driver of a blue tractor and the winner of a Blue Ribbon.

When I noticed the two visitors I naturally stopped work and went over to talk to them. Their mission was to invite me back with them to Italy to study opera and be a professional singer. I was flattered. But I knew right then what my answer would be. But in order that I should not appear too discourteous I told them that I would let them know in a few days' time. And I turned down the offer that would have changed my life.

Now I had the little matter of the National to take care of, and the ambition of winning a second Blue Ribbon. I had a month to prepare for the festival, which was to be held at Ammanford. One of the set pieces was *Lenski's Aria* from Tchaikovsky's *Eugene Onegin*. And I hadn't even looked at it.

The prelim at Ammanford duly arrived and I was pretty pleased with my performance. And out of 30 competitors I was chosen as one of three to appear on stage. The competition was to be held on the Friday morning and I was marked 96 out of a possible hundred on the Aria and 93 on *Y Dieithryn*. Following my success, the BBC asked me to sing live on television that evening. But I had to refuse as I had to return home to do the milking. So they recorded me instead.

On Saturday evening I had finished the milking early so that I could make it in time for the Blue Ribbon event. Also appearing in the final would be Marian Roberts, soprano; Ken Jones, bass; Mabel Roberts, contralto; Laura Hughes, mezzo; myself, tenor and Tom Evans, Gwanas, and Nigel Watkins, baritones. History was made because for the first time ever, seven would appear in the Blue Ribbon event. The judges in the baritone competition couldn't separate Tom and Nigel.

The adjudicators in the final were Trefor Anthony, Sir Geraint Evans and Meirion Williams. Yes, I won the Blue Ribbon. But I lost my music bag. And I can remember Alun Williams announcing that Dai Jones Llanilar had lost his bag. 'It's brown,' said Alun, 'and his music sheets are in it. And I wouldn't be at all surprised if his milking instructions are in it as well.'

The loss of the bag was a minor irritation. I had won the Blue Ribbon. And I had shared a record. At 26 years old it made me and Stuart Burrows the two youngest soloists ever to win the coveted award. Having won, Selwyn Roderick from the BBC invited me back to sing in the Gymanfa Ganu the following night. And singing Osborne Roberts's *Y Nefoedd* (Heaven) was indeed heaven with the huge pavilion packed solid.

Behind all this there lies an interesting little anecdote. Having won the tenor solo competition on the Friday I stopped on my way home to buy take-away fish and chips in Llandeilo. There in the restaurant was Aled Lloyd Davies, a seasoned *eisteddfodwr* and singer. He had just visited the historical Carreg Cennen Castle a few miles away. He congratulated me on my success and I told him how nervous I felt facing the Blue Ribbon event. He gave me great heart by telling me not to worry because all of Wales would be behind me. And I know for certain that Aled's words lifted me.

But I must have been nervous. Not only did I order cod and chips, I also ordered mushy peas, which I hate. On top of that they're not the easiest of foods to eat in the car when you're driving. I have never driven through Llandeilo after that night without quietly thanking Aled. I'm sure he helped me. Mushy peas also come to mind.

The last time I ever competed at an eisteddfod was at Ponterwyd. Having won the Blue Ribbon on the Saturday, the Ponterwyd eisteddfod was on the following Friday, as it always has been. It was Geraint Howells, who later became Lord Geraint of Ponterwyd, who persuaded me to compete. He was the secretary, and remained so until the Eisteddfod ceased to be a few years ago. And now, Geraint himself has gone. I shall always remember the last piece I ever sang competitively. It was an extract from Haydn's *Creation*, with Dr Llifon Hughes Jones adjudicating. That was to be my last eisteddfod. And yes, I won.

The eisteddfod stage is the best place in the world for someone to serve his apprenticeship if he is determined to be an entertainer in Wales. If you want to entertain a Welsh audience, then you have to know how to go about entertaining them. It helps if your roots are deep in the soil of the heartland. It helps if you can come up with a ready but tasteful retort. You also have to know how to treat people, how to read an audience.

And that was undoubtedly one of the greatest lessons I was ever taught by Ifan Maldwyn, my first elocution tutor. Yes, Redvers Llewellyn and Colin Jones were two geniuses who themselves had passed on their craft to others, the craft of giving voice, of producing that voice. But Ifan Maldwyn taught me the most important gift of all, how to deal with people. His argument was always this, 'If a poet is a good poet, and if you can express that poetry, you are giving to your audience what it craves. And if you manage to give an audience what it craves, you will never be out of work.'

And he also told me something that might be even more important. 'Remember, if you persevere, you will become someone. Remember also that when you do become someone, you might get to talk to a king. But you must always be humble enough as well to talk to a beggar.'

And if I ever learnt anything at all, I did learn that. As long as people have a conscience, their status means nothing to me.

7

All the World's Stage

Following my double Blue Ribbon success at Llangollen and Ammanford, invitations to sing in various concerts began to pour in. And this presented a new problem. Now I needed a repertoire. Up until then, when I had occasionally performed on the concert stage, there would be a compère who would introduce me. Now I needed to be able to project to the audience my own personality. So this was quite a venture and a challenge.

The first thing I did, having realized that taking this new direction would mean even more travelling, was to change my car for a better model. All my previous cars had been bought second-hand. So I bought a Cortina 1600GT. And yes, I do remember its registration number. It was LEJ 101 J. And as a result of my ever-increasing bookings I subsequently changed my car every year. I changed the Cortina for an Austin 1800 S, and its registration was NEJ 864 K. That was a huge car, as large as some of the halls where I'd performed. And like William Ty'n Llwyn's car, it would pass everything except a petrol pump. I changed that particular car after 11 months with 93,000 miles on its clock.

At the height of my concert career I would make around 80 appearances annually. And to add extra pressure I also acted as my own agent. As a result I would fill my own diary. It was up to me whether to accept a booking or refuse it. It was hard work. And during all this time I had to persist with my training. The voice is as important to a singer as fitness is to an athlete. If you're a sprinter, for example, a boxer or a golfer, you have to train. The same is true of an instrumentalist in an orchestra. Training is essential. And it's no different being a soloist.

In the meantime, following the death of Ifan Maldwyn, my mentor, Eiluned Douglas Williams had taken me under her wing. She was known in eisteddfodic circles as *Eiluned o Lŷn,* and much of my subsequent success was due to her. I would visit her home, Pennant, Dolgellau, twice a week to concentrate on elocution. And I still visited Colin Jones in Rhos every Sunday.

In the various concerts it was inevitable that I would sing with different accompanists. And the relationship between the singer and his accompanist can be extremely important. In the event I was very fortunate to have, on a fairly regular basis, such accomplished accompanists as Eiluned and Colin. They rate among the best that Wales has ever boasted. They would always be there should I encounter a particularly difficult passage. Should I show a lack of confidence, they would always strengthen me. And I can honestly state that a good accompanist amounts to 60 per cent of the performance.

Most of the big stars believe that it is preferable to sing with an orchestra. They feel that an orchestra adds more substance to a performance. But to me a good accompanist is all-important. Unfortunately we do not possess all that many in Wales. An accompanist does not merely play the notes, faithfully following the copy. An accompanist lives the performance with you. And that is why so many soloists retain their own personal pianist.

Among those early invitations were many from Welsh

societies from outside Wales. I suppose that they would regularly study the list of winners in the various eisteddfodau before choosing the artistes for their annual concerts. I would go as far afield as Sheffield, Leeds, Manchester, Birmingham, Liverpool and London. Then there were trips abroad to Canada, the USA and Africa.

Strange as it may seem, the bigger the venue, the better the audience appreciated the country humour. It was so different to that which they were used to. I soon came to realize that they welcomed the occasional funny story between songs. Then I would add a little bit of clowning while performing in a duet. This was always possible with songs like *Gendarmes*. I would sing in a funny voice and make all sorts of silly gestures and the audience would love it. In short, I aimed at creating my own personal style.

This clowning was especially appropriate when I would share the stage with a woman. I was once appearing with Nansi Richards in St Clears when Beti Lewis-Fisher was accompanying us. Nansi and I were performing the old Welsh favourite *Hywel a Blodwen*. The copy was rather torn and tattered and just for devilment I pocketed the last page and handed Beti the rest of the pages. Beti played beautifully, as she always did, but she had to finish prematurely. She jumped on her feet in panic.

'I haven't got all the music!' she blurted out. 'I haven't got all the music!'

I went to my pocket, took out the missing page and handed it to Beti. The audience was in fits of laughter while poor Nansi, her face as red as a tomato, waved her fist at me while calling me every name under the sun.

I was privileged to appear with a host of singers, almost all of them Welsh, many of them performing professionally.

And I would be invited to perform in various oratorios and short operas throughout Wales. There was a strong operatic society in Aberystwyth and I was invited there to play Rudolfo in *La Boheme.* I also played *The Beggars' Opera.*

I enjoyed playing *The Beggars' Opera* in particular. The producer was the late Alwyn Jones, who was the education officer in the county at the time. He was much involved in the theatre. His brother, Gwynne Hughes Jones, was the county's drama organizer. Both of them were very supportive when I started out as a concert singer.

Gwynne once tried to teach me the importance of deportment. 'Damn it, Dai,' he told me, 'you should learn how to walk on stage. You tend to walk with your head down and your bum pushed back. With you it's a case of "watch my head, my arse is coming".'

I was a member of the cast in the pageant that Gwynne produced in the Cardigan National Eisteddfod where I played one of the main characters. There, for the first time ever, I sang *penillion,* a counterpoint style that is unique to Wales. And I must say, I enjoyed the experience.

But it was Alwyn, Gwynne's brother, who produced *The Beggars' Opera.* And in it I played Filtch. Richard Rees, who was a great friend and a hero, played MacHeath, the highwayman. Filtch was his manservant. It came to the dress rehearsal with all the cast dressed up in their costumes and wearing their make-up. It was a Sunday, and I decided halfway through to disappear. Noticing my absence Alwyn called out for me. 'Filtch, Filtch, where are you, damn you?'

'Sorry, Alwyn,' said Dic Rees. 'He's gone home to do the milking.'

Alwyn couldn't believe it. But it was true. I was driving home through Llanilar in my costume and make-up, which consisted mostly of black grease-paint, just as members of the congregation were reaching Carmel chapel. And I could imagine them staring in bewilderment trying to work out who the hell was driving Dai Berthlwyd's car?

I parked in the farm-yard and went down to fetch the cows. And things got worse. As usual, the Jersey cow was the first to the gate. But when she saw me in my costume she ran as if all the hounds of hell were snapping at her heels. And she didn't return until the following morning.

In the same opera Dic, as MacHeath, was captured towards the end. And there he stood on a box with the rope around his neck just before his execution. I was meant to enter with the words, 'My heart grieves for you, Captain'. But I just couldn't remember the words. And even if someone had threatened me with a gun, I couldn't have found the right words. There I stood, doing my very best to recall the words. But what came out was, 'All the best, Captain'. It should have been a sombre moment. But the audience was in fits.

Then, in *La Boheme,* with the soprano Anelma Jones from Tywyn playing Mimi, and I the part of Rudolfo, we came to the last act where she dies in my arms. I should have sung the words, 'O God, Mimi . . .!' But I sang 'Oh Christ, Mimi . . .' Conducting the orchestra during the final rehearsal was Professor Ian Parrott. And he corrected me. 'It's supposed to be "Oh God",' he said. 'Never mind,' I retorted, 'same family.'

I performed my first *Messiah* down in Risca with the Maestro himself, Glynne Jones Pendyrus conducting. I knew Glynne very well having toured America and Canada for three weeks with the Pendyrus Male Voice Choir. That venture was memorable for many reasons, one of them being that the flight from Rhoose Airport was my first-ever experience of flying. Not only that, I was on the inaugural charter flight from the airport. It was a terrifying experience.

We should have left at ten o'clock in the morning, but bad weather held us up for twelve hours. There was a plentiful supply of beer and other stronger beverages on board, more than enough to last the return flight to California, which meant flying for fifteen hours one-way. We stopped over in Iceland for an hour on the way over, and by then the bar was dry. The whole stock had lasted three hours when it should have lasted for thirty hours.

Sitting next to me was another passenger who was, like me, making his maiden flight. Not only that, at 70 years old he had never left home before. But his family had persuaded him to take the opportunity of going with the choir. And he was quite an eccentric. He absolutely refused to use the plane's toilet because there were no curtains on the cubicle windows. Who was going to be able to see him through that window at 30,000 feet, apart from God, well God himself only knows.

Having arrived safely we were all dining out one night in a posh restaurant, and the old boy sat next to me. Despite the fact that he was missing all his teeth he decided to order a steak. The waitress asked him how he would like his steake. His answer, in all innocence, was, 'On a plate, please.'

That tour was an unforgettable experience. And Glynne was lording it and loving it all. Glynne was a marvellous character. He once stormed out of an eisteddfod at Boduan near Pwllheli after spotting a modulator on the stage. He hated *sol-fah*. And while adjudicating in the Strata Florida eisteddfod he decided to draw an analogy between the various singers and different meals. The best soloist he compared to caviar. And down he went through a turkey dinner and to the very bottom to a local singer, Iorrie Williams.

'And now,' said Glynne, 'how shall I compare Iorrie? Well, here we come to the mashed potatoes and gravy.'

The tour took us through the Rockies. Travelling with the choir was Harvard Gregory, who was the compère, and Aeronwy, Dylan Thomas's daughter who was there to read her father's work. She later married one of the choir members, Trefor Ellis.

We visited Edmonton and New York. Niagara Falls as well. And we saw many of the wonders of those two huge countries. While in Toronto I was awakened one morning by a knock on my bedroom door. It was a member of staff asking me whether I'd be prepared to meet a visitor. I readily agreed and in walked John Williams, an elderly man who was an exile from the Caernarfon area. He lived in New York State with his sister, where he farmed 300 dairy cows. He had read in his local paper that a choir from Wales would be visiting. And he felt so homesick that he travelled up to Toronto in the hope of meeting someone from the old country. He spent the whole day in my company and he was so grateful that if I had asked him for half of the city, he would have willingly given it to me.

He was naturally eager to hear some news of Caernarfon. And thanks to all the competing I had done over the years I knew of places like Rhostryfan, Nebo, Nant Peris and Llanrug. As I mentioned these place-names the tears were rolling down his cheeks. And he begged me, 'Name them again.' He wanted me to relate those place-names over and over again, so as to remind him of what he had left behind.

The first stop was San Francisco, where we spent four nights. By a happy coincidence, Stuart Burrows and Sir

Geraint Evans, who were appearing in opera, were there as well. And they took us out to an up-market hotel where they treated us royally on our first night. During that evening, Stuart Burrows approached me and asked me to consider adapting my repertoire to include some of the old Welsh favourites.

'If the Americans want opera, they'll go to the opera house,' he said. 'If they want *Lieder,* they'll go to a recital. But if they've come along to listen to a singer from Wales, then they'll naturally expect songs from Wales as well.'

I took his advice and changed my programme. And I will be eternally grateful to him for his wise words. I sang *Arafa Don* (Wave, Abate) and *Y Ferch o Blwy Penderyn* (The Girl from the Parish of Penderyn). And when I sang *Bugeilio'r Gwenith Gwyn* (Tending the White Wheat), I had the audience in the palm of my hand.

The only burden was the travelling. Moving from state to state. Flying, travelling by train. Once we were put up in the most imposing hotel in the world. But the snag was that we didn't arrive till the early hours of the morning. The bed was so huge and soft that I virtually disappeared into it. Unfortunately I had to be up again within two hours.

We visited Wyoming. And there, on the inside of the hotel bedroom door was a sign warning us not to venture out alone but to travel in groups. Ifor Lloyd and I shared a room and during the night we could literally hear guns being fired on the street. We visited a nearby bar where the barman sent the pints sliding along the counter just like a scene from a John Wayne movie.

We visited Chicago only to see the same warning signs telling us to travel in groups. So out we went, all 120 of us walking down the street together. We hadn't walked far before three police cars screeched to a halt opposite us. Out jumped half-a-dozen officers. Bristling with guns, they asked us where we were going? Glynne Jones tried to explain that we were a Welsh choir and that we were out for a pint. Not being completely convinced, they followed us to a bar where they lined up across the doorways with their hands hovering rather too close to their guns for my liking. Then Glynne broke the deadlock.

'Right,' he ordered us, 'all together, sing *Myfanwy* . . . one, two three . . .'

Within seconds the cops had doffed their caps and the tears were running down their cheeks as they listened to the singing. And the bar-keeper was so impressed, he paid for a drink for us all. Quite an expensive round when you consider how many of us were there.

The Welsh exiles flocked to the concerts. In San Francisco there was an audience of 12,500. I was, almost literally, scared stiff. The stage manager realized how nervous I was and tried to console me. And I explained to him that back home in Wales I was just an ordinary small farmer and that something like this was totally alien to me. There I was, I explained, facing a massive audience and all of them complete strangers.

'I'll give you some free advice,' he said. 'Now if, as you say you are, nothing more than an ordinary small farmer who is feeling nervous about facing thousands of strangers, look at them exactly as you would if you were looking over the hedge at a field of cabbages.'

And that's what I did. And it worked.

I'd like to return to America sometime on a more leisurely visit without the distraction of performing or filming. But because of the work-load I have to deal with it's proved impossible so far. But perhaps the chance will come someday.

Most bookings, naturally, were back in Wales. I would help organize an annual concert in Llanilar on the first Friday in November to raise money for the local show. Because of my connections I have been able to attract some of the biggest names in Wales for a moderate fee. One year the guest singer was Tom Davies, Bryniog. He arrived early one afternoon so that he could visit Berthlwyd to have a look at the sheep and cattle. And being a farmer himself he appreciated the ducks that we kept there. I presented him with two ducks as well as a sheepdog pup. He placed the ducks in a box in the back of his Toyota pickup leaving the dog free inside.

We arrived at the concert at Carmel chapel all dolled up in our dickey bows. I had just introduced Tom to the audience when we heard a strange noise, 'quack-quack-quack'. But I couldn't remember Chapel House ever keeping ducks. Then we heard it again 'Quack-quack-quack'. Out I went and there, in the back of Tom's pickup, the pup had managed to free the ducks from their box and was chasing them all around the back of the Toyota. That, as far as I know, was the only time for Tom to perform accompanied by two ducks.

I would sometimes travel down to London to perform. I once sang in the Albert Hall when Alun Williams was the compère. And Alun has played a leading part in my career. Yes, those old coincidences again. He gave me the first chance to appear on television. He was the compère at Llangollen when I won the Blue Ribbon, at Ammanford when I did the double, and after Alun died, which was a great loss to Welsh broadcasting and entertainment in general, I inherited his Sunday night radio request programme.

That night at the Albert Hall, Dic Rees and I sang a duet in what was a live televised concert. The following Monday I was down in Llangwrddon chatting to Stephen y Felin. The programme had gone out live and Stephen had seen it.

'Well, Dai,' he said, 'I enjoyed you singing on the television last night. Damn, you sang well.'

'Thank you,' I said.

'And Dai *bach*, damn it, you looked smart. You looked a real gent in your shit-through jacket.'

That was Stephen's description of a tail-coat.

I was privileged to be among the first group of Welsh singers to perform at the Lagos Welsh Society's Saint David's Day concert in Nigeria. We went out as a quartet, Dic Rees, Pennal, Iona Jones from London, Margaret Lewis Jones, Llanbryn-mair and I. The *Western Mail* gave the story some considerable publicity. And shortly before we left for Nigeria I was at Tregaron mart when Davies Pengarreg stopped to talk to me.

'Well, well,' he said, 'I see that you're going out to sing to the Blacks in Africa.'

'No, no, not to the Blacks,' I explained. 'We'll be singing for the Lagos Welsh Society.'

'Oh, I see," said Davies. "You mean to say they've got Welsh Blacks out in Africa?'

We had a great time out in Lagos. It was just after the military coup. We flew out of Heathrow on a bitterly cold day. It was the end of February and I was wearing a thick Aran sweater with its collar turned up over my ears. Out we went from the plane at Lagos airport to a temperature of over 100 degrees.

As the coup had just happened, we all felt rather nervous. But we were treated like royalty. We stayed with a Welsh family who had spent some time in America before moving to Nigeria. Their youngest daughter was called Wendy. And one night, in a blind panic, I had to call her to my bedroom.

'Wendy, come quick! There's an alligator on the wall!'

She dashed over immediately only to burst out laughing. The creature crawling up the wall was a lizard. But to someone like me who is afraid of cats, it looked as big as an alligator.

We would rehearse every morning with our accompanist, Carol. She was married to a Welshman. During the afternoon it would be too hot to do anything so we had a break before performing in the evening. When I returned from Lagos I had to throw away my suit. Because of the heat, my perspiration had stiffened it to such an extent it felt like cardboard.

While we were out there we were given the opportunity of singing with a local choir made up of black singers who had won at Llangollen. It was an incredible experience.

Among the Welsh exiles living in Lagos was Elwyn Williams and his wife Rona. He was the head of one of the local banks out there. One night we were treated to a feast and, during the dinner, Elwyn clapped his hands and called one of the attendants, who was known to everyone as Friday. There was a parrot in the dining room, and its constant chattering was disturbing everyone.

'Friday,' said Elwyn, 'see to that parrot.'

Friday removed the bird and we resumed eating in peace. The following night we had another feast, this time a chicken dinner. And Elwyn complimented Friday on the meal.

'Lovely chicken,' he said.

'That was not chicken, sir,' said Friday. 'That was parrot.'

Yes, Friday had misunderstood Elwyn, and had killed and roasted the parrot. Even worse was the fact that Elwyn was only looking after the bird for one of his friends. So he went out and bought a parrot that looked something like the ex-parrot hoping his friend wouldn't notice the difference. But that very night he placed the cage too near an electric cable. The new parrot peeled away the plastic cover and was electrocuted.

That was the difficulty in Lagos. You never really knew what you were eating. One night in a restaurant, Dic couldn't understand why he could hear strange rattling sounds coming from his plate as he ate. It was pretty dark there so he lit a match. And there in front of him he saw snails' shells.

Visiting Lagos proved to be a completely different experience from anything I had encountered before. The markets were like ant-hills with people milling around the stalls looking for bargains, mostly handbags and other leather goods. Also popular were the long traditional colourful native dresses. Dic and I bought one each to take home. And the first thing I told Olwen, when I returned was that I had bought her an Afghan.

'An Afghan?' she said. 'What in the world will I do with that? And anyway, how did you manage to smuggle it through customs? Have you been to see the vet?'

'Vet? What do you mean?'

'Well, if you've bought me an Afghan, you'll have to take the dog to the vet and leave it in quarantine.'

'Dog? It's a dress, not a dog.'

'You stupid idiot," said Olwen. "What you've bought is a kaftan, not an Afghan.'

8

Marriage Games

My association with the media, although I had already dipped my feet in the water, as it were, really took off in 1970 when I began presenting *Siôn a Siân,* the Welsh-language version of *Mr & Mrs*. And it all came about through a misunderstanding on my part.

I had appeared on various shows both on the BBC and HTV. This was when every department could boast its own producer. At HTV, for instance, Esme Lewis was the musical producer, and a singing audition was essential before appearing on the screen. This would mean singing various songs and securing Esme's approval before you could appear on the screen.

It was Ieuan Davies who invited me down to HTV in Cardiff to discuss the possibility of presenting *Siôn a Siân*. That, at least, was what I thought he had said. I had seen the game show without taking all that much interest in it. At that time it was fronted by I.B. Griffith and Jenny Ogwen.

We settled on a date – I think it was a Wednesday – and the previous night I was appearing in concert at Birchgrove near Swansea with the Gyrlais Choir. I stayed there overnight and travelled on to Cardiff the following day. And as I drove eastward I wondered what lay in store for me. But as soon as I arrived I realized that I had, in my innocence, misread the situation. What I was attending was not a meeting with Ieuan Davies but an audition. I was ready to turn on my heels and go home. But being a good Cardi I decided that I would eat first and then go home. And I went to the canteen.

There I was told that the auditions had been held all morning and that more potential-presenters would be auditioned during the afternoon. And that's when I decided at least to have a go. But having entered the studio I was again tempted to leave. There, awaiting their turn, were some well-known faces from television, stars that appeared weekly on the screen. I had, by now, abandoned all hope.

My turn came and all I was asked to do for the audition was to open and close the programme. I had to welcome the imaginary audience, initiate a short dialogue with Jenny Ogwen and close the programme. And that was it.

As I was leaving I was thanked by Ieuan for showing an interest. I explained to him my misreading of the situation and that I had not expected an audition. In my naïvety I had expected to be offered the job. Ieuan smiled and explained that I would be told of his decision in good time. To me it seemed like the old story of 'don't call us, we'll call you'. And that was it.

I drove home. At that time the distance between Llanilar and Cardiff seemed much longer. And my misreading of the situation made it seem longer still. But the following morning I was stunned when I took a call from Ieuan offering me the job. Needless to say, I accepted immediately. Within a week a letter arrived from the man I was replacing, I.B. Griffith, one of the kindest letters I have ever received. He had heard that I had been offered the job of presenting the show and he wished me every success. I treasured that letter. It was a great incentive for me.

I presented *Siôn a Siân* for 17 years and during that time I sang over 700 songs on the series. We would record two shows a day to begin with. And after the first show was transmitted we received a letter from a viewer suggesting that it was a waste having me as presenter without asking me to sing. Ieuan accepted the suggestion on condition that I received requests from viewers. I immediately agreed to this. To me it was more important than offering prizes on the show. Nowadays, of course, prizes are an integral part of any game show. They are the bait that tempts viewers to watch.

I first sang at the end of the third show and then asked the viewers for their requests. The response was amazing. Letters from all parts of Wales flooded in, and Janice Ball was invited to join us as the accompanist making us a team of three, Janice, Jenny and myself.

Throughout my 17 years I worked with various co-presenters making it seem as if I had more wives than Henry the Eighth. Jenny did two stints with me. Then there was Sara Tudor from Anglesey. She was followed by Rosalind Lloyd. And when she left, Mair Rowlands took over for a while. Jenny then returned and left for the second time. And she was replaced, in turn, by Mari Emlyn. And Mari was my last co-presenter.

Janice Ball, however, stayed throughout. And she was a very special accompanist. She seemed to understand how I felt. Should I be suffering from a bad cold she would play in a lower key. Should I be in good form she would play in a higher key, especially if the song was a lively one.

What made it difficult on the show was that we were working to a very tight schedule. If we were running over time, two or three verses would have to be chopped, and that would have to be done sensibly and sensitively. We would never know how we stood until the show was recorded. That meant that I occasionally had to take advantage of an idiot-board. An idiot-board was a large board with the words of the song written on it in large letters. It would be held up in front of the singer or presenter. The advent of the autocue, where words appear on a small screen fixed to the front of the camera lens, made it redundant. Having to read from the idiot-board was a frightening experience, and I would rather have done without it.

When Eifion Lloyd Jones took over as producer he would, because of the shortage of original songs, write Welsh words to popular tunes. But more often than not I would not see the words until the morning of the recording. That meant an extra obstacle. As well as having to rehearse the movements, the timing and the chat, I had to try to learn the words of the song as well. And this, remember, would happen twice a day.

The floor manager was Henry Chambers Jones. From the corner of my eye I would often see him jumping up and down urging me on. That would be a sure sign that the recording was running too long. But he enjoyed doing this so much that he would sometimes forget himself completely.

It was Henry who held up the idiot-board when that became necessary. On one occasion I had two verses to sing. I knew the words of the first verse fairly well. But when Henry raised the board with the words of the second verse he held it upside-down. I had to stop. Thank God it wasn't a live show. But it gave me the opportunity to bait him.

'You silly fool, Henry. Why didn't you hold the board the right way up?'

'If you could do something as simple as learning the words, you wouldn't need me at all,' answered Henry.

Those were good times at HTV. We would record the shows in the Pontcanna studio. But during the summer months, should the weather allow it, we would shoot the shows on a set built in the open air on the lawn. At that time, all of us involved would flock to the company's social club. There we would mix freely with the bosses and executives. Aled Vaughan was the head of HTV at the time. Then there was Euryn Ogwen, who was a production director, Geraint Rees, Ieuan Davies, Dorothy Williams and Jean Parry Jones. We were all one big happy family.

There was only one changing room, and Jenny and I had to share it. Then we would go to make-up. Here again everyone knew everyone else, all on first-name terms. Then, when everything was over, we would all meet up in the club. It was more a friendship club than anything else. And Aled Vaughan would be available at any time to discuss any problem.

For a short period we recorded the show up in the Mold studios with Dorothy Williams directing. But that didn't last long. Cardiff was the show's true home.

Presenting *Siôn a Siân* was another perfect opportunity to meet people. And despite this new direction I was still performing some 80 concerts a year. Then the television show widened its appeal by becoming a stage production as well. A venue would be chosen, and Jenny, Janice and I, together with the whole production team, would present an evening performance. All the costs would be met by HTV and the profits would go towards a local charity.

This new venture was first tried out in St Clears, in the Ysgol Griffith Jones school hall. It was a sweeping success. We had four married couples competing and whether they won or not, they received a clock as a memento. To stretch the evening out I sang after the appearance of every pair. Jenny would also present an item and Janice would perform a piano solo. And of course, I would throw in a sprinkling of jokes.

At the end of these stage shows I would raffle one of the clocks used as prizes. Every night this would raise between £80 and £100. That money would be presented to the local treasurer to be passed on to a deserving cause.

I owe a great debt to *Siôn a Siân*. It was as a direct result of my experience of compèring the show that I went on to present dozens, indeed hundreds, of concerts and variety shows. It gave me the opportunity of introducing people and to talk to competitors and audiences throughout Wales. And the stage shows in particular gave audiences the opportunity, in their own localities, to enjoy themselves. And most importantly to me, I was able to maintain a rapport with these audiences.

I firmly believed that the media missed out on a golden opportunity here. They should have made more use of local halls and theatres. They were the ideal locations for staging and recording shows like *Siôn a Siân* with local competitors appearing in front of their own people.

We staged shows throughout Wales, north, south and central. And they were memorable events. People began to invite us to their localities. That great character Dic Davies, who appeared with Dathan for years on a Welsh-language gardening series on television invited us to Pontargothi. And we accepted his invitation. It attracted so many that dozens had to be turned back at the door. Not only did we entertain the audience, we also raised a considerable sum of money towards the local agricultural show.

An integral part of these stage shows was the research that was done in advance. From friends of the competing couples we would learn various little secrets. This knowledge was then used as a basis for some of the questions. And this would add greatly to the enjoyment.

Through both the studio and stage shows we discovered many great characters. One year we recorded a special Christmas show. Among the competitors were Bertie Stephens and his wife from Llangeitho. We had finished rehearsing and were now recording the actual proceedings. As Mr and Mrs Stephens entered the set Bertie's wife turned to Jenny.

'You take him down, *bach*,' she said. 'I'll be back now. You see, I've forgotten my gloves.'

And off she went.

Occasionally, for variety's sake, we would introduce something different. On one show, Jenny appeared with a row of ties on a tray. The idea was to ask the wife which tie her husband would choose. Then the husband appeared and was asked his opinion.

'Now then,' I asked, 'which of these ties would you wear around your neck?'

He looked a little bemused. And no wonder.

'Damn it,' he said, 'I wouldn't like to wear any of those around my neck.'

Jenny had picked up the wrong tray. On this tray there was a display of belts.

Theoretically it would be possible to cheat on the show. And once we did catch a couple, a respectable couple at that, attempting to deceive. They were caught fair and square and to avoid embarrassment we explained to them that the show would, nevertheless, be televised. But we assured them that we would refrain from publicizing the fact that they had cheated on condition that we withheld the prize-money. They had won the jackpot of £1,000. We even played back the tape of the recording for them in a private room. And yes, they admitted to cheating.

The programme was duly transmitted and all their friends congratulated them on winning the jackpot. But shortly afterwards I happened to be a guest soloist in the very same chapel that the couple attended. And the wife came over to me with a face like thunder.

'I don't want anything more to do with you, Dai Jones,' she said. 'We watched the programme and we couldn't see that we had done anything wrong.'

Of course they hadn't. We had censored the offending scenes. Rather than complain she should have been thankful that we had kept their dark secret. By the way, both of them were chapel deacons.

There was an old chap from the north, the salt of the earth from Eglwys-bach, Conwy, who appeared. And of course, he was given a clock. Five years later I received a letter from him.

'I haven't seen you for some time,' said the letter. 'I sincerely hope that you are keeping well. By the way, the purpose of my letter is this: the clock battery has expired. Could you send me a new one?'

The old battery had lasted for five years. Not bad going. But we did send him a boxful of new batteries, courtesy of HTV.

Sometimes a particular phrase or word would cause me

no end of problems. Once, the word 'chivalry' came up in a question. I don't think I had even heard the word before and I certainly didn't know what it meant. But the biggest problem was pronouncing it. I have problems even now. I just couldn't get my tongue around the word. I pronounced it 'chilvary'. Then it became 'chivelary'. And of course, the more I panicked the worse things got. The audience were in tears of laughter. And in the end the woman I was questioning had to ask the question herself – and answer it.

Another time I asked the wife, 'When your husband comes in from the fields does he leave his boots outside? Does he clean them thoroughly and keep them on? Or does he walk in just as he is?'

That gave her plenty of options. Or so I thought. But no.

'He leaves them in the conservatory,' she said.

That was another new word for me. So I wrote it down on a piece of paper hoping that it would help. But when the husband came on and I had to disclose his wife's answer, I was stumped.

'Your wife tells me that you leave your boots in the conservatives,' I said.

The audience's laughter at my expense gradually became an integral part of the show. And should a competitor slip up it was important for me to seize upon that and turn it into a joke.

I was once questioning a minister's wife. 'What,' I asked, 'would your husband take for a bad cold? Hot milk and an Aspirin? Medication with honey and lemon? Or a tot of whiskey?'

She thought hard for a moment. 'Well,' she said, 'I suppose I'll have to tell the truth whether it will cost me the jackpot or not. He would take a tot of whiskey.'

The One that Got Away! The Royal Welsh says goodbye to my old broadcasting friend, Sulwyn Thomas.

Holding forth in my role as President of the Welsh Black Society.

(courtesy of Arvid Parry Jones)

On the Rocks – like every farmer!

Fodlas Elwyn, winner of the Queen Mother's Cup at Smithfield.

In my Element: crushing grapes in France!

The hostesses on *Siôn a Siân* were never like this!
Filming *Jam Bo Bwana* (S4C).

Royal Approval: being presented to the Queen Mother at Smithfield.

One Dai and his Dog – old Mal on this occasion.

Two Types of Horse Power!
Trotting in Tregaron and
Revving on the Farm.

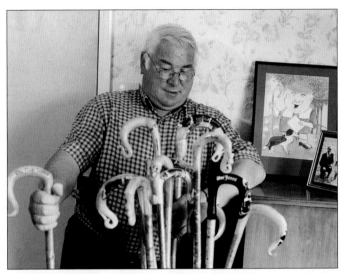

All Crooks Together! *(courtesy of S4C)*

Every Dog has its Dai! On safari with Craig and Mick.

(courtesy of S4C)

A proud Fellow of Bafta Wales. *(courtesy of S4C)*

Like Father, like Son. *(courtesy of S4C)*

'Should I go, Olwen?' Filling the already full Dai-ary!
(courtesy of S4C)

The Loves of my Life – granddaughter, Celine, and the Welsh Blacks!
(courtesy of Arvid Parry Jones)

In Distinguished Company: receiving my Fellowship of the University of Wales from Vice-Chancellor Derec Llwyd Morgan, and the third of my great heroes, Lord Elystan Morgan.

(courtesy of The Cambrian News*)*

At the Royal Welsh Show 2004, receiving the Sir Brynner Jones Award from Prince Charles for my contribution to Welsh Agriculture.

(courtesy of Tegwyn Roberts)

The audience started whispering amongst themselves. And on came the minister. I asked him the same questions. But his answer was, 'Hot milk before going to bed.'

When I revealed to him his wife's answer he looked a little bit sheepish.

'I suppose I should have said that as well,' he admitted, 'because that's the truth.'

Well, unfortunately his little white lie cost him £1,000.

On another occasion the jackpot depended on the answer to the last question which was, 'What kind of pyjamas did your husband wear last night?' The husband had stated that he did not wear pyjamas at all. So I asked her, 'Did he wear a plain one, a flowery one, a striped pair or no pyjamas at all?'

'None at all? Don't be silly,' she said. 'He wore flowery pyjamas.'

And I remember telling her that she could have bought hundreds of pairs for £1,000.

We took the show to Tal-y-bont once. The local press, naturally, was present and a photograph was taken of the four pairs of competitors sporting the clocks they had been presented with. Unfortunately the caption beneath the photograph included a misprint. It should have stated that the *Siôn a Siân* competitors in the photograph were displaying their clocks. Unfortunately the 'l' in 'clocks' was missing.

With all the travelling involved it wasn't always easy to find some of the venues. Sara Tudor and I were heading for Gorseinon one night. She was following the directions on a map. According to Sara, the hall should have been on the left, but we ended up in a tyre salesroom. She was holding the map upside-down.

At another venue, Jenny and Janice had gone to the toilet, an outdoor Elsan closet which stood on a slope. There wasn't a lock on the door so they asked me to keep a lookout. I urged them to hurry things up as it was a cold night. Then I felt my feet warming. But it wasn't because the weather was getting warmer. There was a hole in the cubicle.

Having spent 17 years compèring the show it was no wonder that people referred to me as 'Dai *Siôn a Siân*'. Not only did the show introduce me to television work, it also helped us financially as a family.

As a result of the show I was asked to front other programmes. There was a series on shearing, for example, when the world shearing championship was held at Corwen. I was, of course, a seasoned shearer so I expected the series, *Corwen Shears,* to be quite straightforward. But the world championship was very different to anything I had ever experienced before.

With the producer, Eifion Lloyd Jones, I visited the pavilion and saw all these shearers from different countries. There were the Fagans from New Zealand, the Wilsons from Scotland. And from Wales there were experts like Arwyn Davies, who was a local man, and Brian Davies from Senny Bridge. It was an incredible scene. When I walked in I could swear that I was watching the *Grand National.* The commentator could have taught Michael O'Sullivan a thing or two.

'And he's on the last one now. He's got two strokes left on the left-hand side of this ewe. And he's really going now. It's Fagan all the way. But no, he's being caught by Wilson . . .'

It was unbelievable. And I had to throw myself into the programme without any kind of rehearsal. Incidentally, I have never been able to work to a script. I tend to do

130

everything off the cuff. And this has made life difficult for the sub-titling and dubbing agencies. I would be asked in advance for my script. Well, we don't work that way. What we do instead is to send the finished programme to the translating agencies. It's helpful sometimes to have a draft or outline of a live show. But as far as scripting is concerned, I never have and I never will prepare a script.

Another series I presented was *Tregampau.* It involved different villages competing against each other in song and verse as well as in arts and crafts. Sara Tudor was again my co-presenter and we worked with three adjudicators.

Then there came another short series, *Jambo Bwana,* where I was filmed in the Nasai Mara and the Serengeti in Kenya with Ken Williams. I spent six weeks out there and enjoyed every minute. We first stayed in the Intercontinental Hotel in Nairobi before going out on a camel safari on the Rumaruti. It was an experience I'll never forget. It meant sleeping out on the riverbank in the open air. We would direct the beams of our torches onto the river and see the crocodiles' eyes glistening in the dark. Luckily we were high above the river and the bank was too steep for the creatures to climb.

We pitched tents as well in Kichwatempo. We would pay an attendant a few shillings a day for looking after our tents. But as those tents were all the same shape, size and colour I found it very difficult to remember which one was mine. Fortunately for me a buffalo had left its dung right outside mine so I paid the attendant not to clean up. It marked my tent just as well as if I had hung a sign there with my name on it.

One night we held a party in a valley nearby. We were warned no to venture anywhere without an experienced escort because of the danger from roaming lions. I was escorted there by members of the local tribe. But one of the cameramen left it late and arrived at the party on his own. He was carrying a stick.

'Damn it, you're a very brave man,' I said, 'coming down here on your own.'

'No problem,' he said, 'I've got this stick.'

'Listen, mate,' I said, if a lion got hold of you, that stick would be more use to him. After he'd eaten you he could use it as a toothpick.'

I could hear the roar of the lions and the whinnying of the zebras from my camp bed. And one day we saw an amazing sight which we managed to record on film. A group of lions had cornered a zebra. They moved in and killed it right there in front of us. But the strangest sight of all was the behaviour of the other animals. As the lions feasted they gathered around in a circle waiting for their turn to feed. It reminded me of funerals back home with the closest relatives gathering around the grave and the friends of the deceased forming a circle around them. Within half an hour there was nothing left of the poor zebra, not even a scrap of bone.

The Masai people were very friendly. As were the Sumbulus. We were allowed into their villages without any problems at all. There was little point in offering them money as payment. They bartered in goats. So we would buy goats in the town and carry them out on our roof-racks. On one particularly hot day I felt some wetness. And I thought, thank God, it's raining. But no, it was one of the goats on the roof of the van emptying its bladder. And believe you me, goat's pee is rather pungent. I needed more after-shave than usual that night.

But primitive as life was out in the bush we did manage to shower. Empty oil drums would be filled with water and a fire lit underneath them. Pipes would then run from the barrels to the rear of the tents. There wasn't much water pressure but at least it was hot.

The Intercontinental Hotel in Nairobi was huge. It was practically a town in its own right. But there would be no need to queue for food or anything else. And having stayed there on our way out, the staff knew us all by name when we returned five weeks later. The clerk behind the desk immediately addressed me as Mr Jones. Not only that, but as he handed me the key he remembered the number of my room from my previous stay. They had memories like elephants.

And yes, I did get to see elephants. Indeed, some of them almost killed us. We had gone into the woods on spec and we were surprised by a whole herd. We had to run for it.

Once we spent a whole day looking for an elephant to film. At long last we found one and we filmed and photographed it for as long as we could. But it tired of being a television star and got rather mad at us. Curling its trunk around a tree it tore it up from the roots.

On another occasion we had parked by an earth bank while we discussed our time-table. We had just opened the doors of the van when we felt an almighty crash. It was a wart-hog rushing out of his burrow. And it left a huge dent in the side of the van.

I flew in a balloon over the Masai Mara. We lifted off at five o'clock in the morning before the animals had awoken. It was a wonderful and eerie experience. And what a sight. As the animals gradually woke up we flew silently above them, zebras, wildebeests and lions. We saw them stirring and prowling in the early morning light. The only sound was the hissing of the gas into the balloon.

There were five of us in the basket, the cameraman and sound man, Ken, myself and the pilot. The basket, when it descended, landed on its side on the edge of an elephant dung-hill. And believe you me, when an elephant leaves its calling card it is no small matter. It defecates by the barrow-load. The only unlucky member of the crew was the sound-man. He landed head-first in it. There he was, up to his shoulders in dung. Luckily he still had his head-phones on or he would have lost his sense of hearing permanently.

Following the balloon flight – there were five balloons in all – we enjoyed a champagne breakfast. It was a slap-up fry-up with gallons of champagne to accompany it. I felt like a king. I have never felt so privileged. There I was being feasted in the most exciting country in the world – and being paid for it as well.

That was not my first balloon flight. I suffered a terrible experience in one while filming in Carmarthenshire. With me was Eirian from Llanwrda, who was known as 'Eirian AD Clad' because he owned a company of the same name. We ascended gracefully only to land in a tree by the village chapel. That evening we had planned to fly from Llangadog Common up towards Llandovery and Cynghordy. But the gas ran out. And when the gas runs out, the balloon comes down. There was no wind to float us, and we barely hovered above the electric power lines and pylons. We were so close that we could hear the electric current humming just below us. I was so terrified that I considered jumping out. As we passed over the film crew, Geraint Rees, the director was standing on a hedge-bank.

'Dai,' he shouted, 'we've got enough film now. You can come down.'

And I shouted back, 'I've had enough too. And I'd only be too glad to come down if I could.'

Fortunately and miraculously a breeze blew from

134

somewhere and carried us from among the pylons and dropped us in the middle of a flock of Beulah sheep. The Beulahs are not my favourite breed by any stretch of the imagination. But I've never been so glad to see a flock of Beulahs.

The balloon flight was filmed for *Cefn Gwlad.* But I have also been privileged to work on various other series. From the very beginning I have compèred shows in the *Noson Lawen* series, a variety show held in barns across the country. Over the years I have also fronted New Year's Eve events, once from Glasgow where I joined Welsh exiles and wore a kilt.

For the past few years I have presented *Rasus*, which is now in its twelfth season. I love working on this live show which televises trotting races from Tir Prince near Abergele. Over the years I have been interested in horse races. I have attended meetings regularly at Llan-non and Tregaron, Blaenpennal and Talgarreg – and I've cheered on, and had the occasional bet on, such famous Welsh horses as Black Bess, Cock o' the North, Lyn Direct, April Morn, and Pilot, a horse from Tregaron. All the various names have remained on the tip of my tongue.

Then S4C came up with the idea of presenting a weekly trotting meeting live. And from its inception it has been a great success. Its secret lies in the fact that it is a natural country activity. Many of us have had our fill of rugby, soccer and cricket. The only sporting activity I can bear to watch is tennis. But as for horse racing, it's remarkable. S4C is the only television channel in Britain to cover trotting, and again it's been a privilege to be a part of it.

As well as appearing live from Tir Prince I have covered trotting as far afield as New Zealand, Germany and France. And, more recently, the USA and Canada.

135

The live show from Tir Prince is quite a challenge. The hour-long programme demands discipline and a good memory, which I can't always boast. You also need to be prepared to expect the unexpected. But again, as in so many activities I have been part of, it gives me the opportunity to meet people from the agricultural world. And those that frequent trotting meetings seem to have a little bit more devilment about them, people who like a bet now and then.

Rasus has also given me the opportunity to meet up again with an old friend from my school-days, John Watkin from Aberystwyth, whose television company is responsible for filming the series. And it also gave me the chance to meet one of the youngest directors in Wales, Geraint Lewis whose father, Rhys, has a long and distinguished track record in filming country pursuits.

As in other shows, there is no shortage of fun in filming *Rasus*. I was doing a promo – an advert for the programme – with a young couple and their children one day. Having seen me on the screen I became quite the hero for the children and they followed me everywhere. At the end of the filming I asked to use the toilet. And one of the kids, who was about seven years old, took me there. It was a modern toilet with a bidet.

'Well, you are lucky,' I said, 'you've got two toilets.'

'No,' he answered and pointed to the bidet, 'that one's Mam's.'

And here I must recall my visit to Munich to film the World Trotting Championship. This was a memorable trip, especially my return journey. I arrived at the airport all packed and ready to go. I went to the check-in counter to show my ticket. But I just couldn't find my passport. I remembered placing it earlier with my credit cards in the side pocket of my suitcase. But the passport and the cards had disappeared. And now I was stuck. I wouldn't be allowed to board the plane.

Together with Geraint Lewis and Hywel Davies – an ex-Grand National winner – I went to the security area. I think Hywel was even more worried than I was. I couldn't see any notices on the walls. And I had a strange feeling that I was in the wrong place. All I could see was a line of doors. Alongside one door there was a row of switches and a large red button. Getting more desperate by the minute, I pressed the red button. The door opened and in we went. Immediately there came the screeching of sirens and a group of uniformed guards surrounded us. One of them was a woman who looked like a refugee from *Cell Block H*. And suddenly all the guards were brandishing guns.

The woman seemed to be the boss. But I couldn't understand one word. Then one of the others pushed his way forward.

'Why you push button?' he asked.

'Well,' I said, 'that was the only button that would open the door.'

'Oh, I see. Come.'

And I was escorted to a desk where I tried to explain that I had lost my passport. I was asked for proof of my identity. But I had nothing to show them. Now I was really worried, as were Geraint and Hywel.

We were now just 30 minutes from take-off. And we were told that we would have to leave, if at all, on a later plane. Geraint and I told Hywel to go ahead of us. Geraint could have left as well but there was little purpose in that as we had arranged to travel home from Heathrow in the same car.

I rang the hotel in case I had left my passport there. No

luck. I searched through my suitcase again. I went through every item of clothing, even my shirts and under-pants. No luck. A bundle of socks dropped on the floor and a man in a turban, walking by, accidentally kicked them across the room. I had to run over to retrieve them.

At last, after what seemed an eternity, an official took us through to the plane. There he explained my predicament to another official. We were told we could now leave on condition that we reported to the police on our arrival.

Off we went at long last. And I was now convinced that my passport and bank cards had been stolen. Yet I could distinctly remember putting them away in the suitcase pocket. Being a good Cardi, I had already phoned home to cancel the cards.

At Heathrow we cleared everything with the police and in the bus that ferried us to the car park I was still discussing my loss with Geraint. I looked once more in the suitcase pocket. There was nothing there except odds and ends, including my mobile phone connection. Then, with the case on my lap, I opened it. And I turned to Geraint.

'Guess what I've found?'

'No,' said Geraint, 'it can't be, can it?'

It was. There, in a neat bundle, was my passport. My credit cards were there as well. Geraint laughed until the tears were rolling down his cheeks. The other passengers looked a little bewildered at all this.

'Think of all the fuss, Geraint,' I said. 'I was almost shot and the bloody passport was here all the time.'

I had panicked, I suppose, and had overlooked it. But it had been a nightmare. Not only had I been in danger of being shot. Even worse, my underpants had been exhibited for all to see in Munich Airport. Not a pretty sight, believe me.

138

9

Country Matters

Towards the end of my long stint on *Siôn a Siân* I began fronting *Cefn Gwlad*. For a while, both series ran simultaneously.

It's difficult to translate the term *Cefn Gwlad*. Like that Welsh word *hiraeth,* there is no literal translation for it. Words like 'rural and 'hinterland' don't convey the true meaning. Neither does 'backwoods'. The nearest word to describe the phrase would probably be the American term, 'heartland'.

At its inception the series had different presenters. Ifor Lloyd presented a few as did Wil Morgan, Norman Closs Parry and Glynog Davies. The format of the programme differed then as well, as some scenes would be shot in the studio. I was approached by Geraint Rees, who has been involved from the very beginning as the series producer, and he asked me whether I'd be interested in doing some presenting. I gladly and eagerly accepted.

Geraint then asked me how I would go about fronting the show. I came up with the idea of filming on my own farm. Geraint could then assess the success or otherwise of the documentary. The finished product pleased him so much that he asked me to come up with another idea.

This was on a Thursday night and he wanted an answer by the following Monday. By Sunday I still hadn't come up with anything. All day I did nothing but think. And late that evening I rang Margaret Hughes, Rhoshaflo, Llanfair Caereinion. I had seen her on one of Hywel Gwynfryn's programmes and she had struck me then as quite a character. One thing that attracted me to the idea was her dialect. It was pure Montgomeryshire.

It was Christmas-time and the traditional *plygain* services, or matins, were being held in the area. And when I rang Margaret she was out attending one of the services. Eventually I managed to contact her and she agreed to take part. But when she heard that we would be there the following day she very nearly changed her mind. So, not counting the programme filmed on my own farm, Margaret became the subject of my very first *Cefn Gwlad*.

That is one of the successes of *Cefn Gwlad*. We never organize a shoot too far in advance. This helps give an impromptu element to the series. So we arranged for the whole crew to meet on the Monday morning in the village. And this kind of arrangement remained for years. The various members of the film crew and I would meet in a central venue, and then we would continue our journey together in a convoy. In those days we would have every one driving different cars, the cameraman, the sound-man, the electrician, then the PA, or production assistant, followed by the producer, and then me. And sometimes, if we needed publicity shots, I would be followed by a photographer.

I remember filming an old drover, Mal Edwards who, coincidentally, lived in the same area as Margaret. And when he saw all the cars he said, 'Hell, don't all park on the farmyard or the neighbours will think that I've died and that it's my funeral today.'

Today, of course, things are very different. The crew is

140

much smaller and the cameraman and sound-man will share a car and all the rest of us will travel in a second car.

Margaret's programme went well, so well that it was extended to two extra episodes, one following her to the Smithfield Show and the other filming her at the Royal Welsh. These, in turn, led to a series which concentrated on characters rather than stories. Then there came a further development with seasonal episodes, such as a Christmas special being shot. Some of these meant overseas visits.

It has become almost a tradition that the shows that please the most are those where I get into difficulties. Or, to put it another way, where I make a right fool of myself. The best example of this, I suppose, would be *Dai ar y Piste* (Dai on the Piste). I had never in my life done any skiing. Since then I have become a competent skier. I won't say I'm brilliant but I can manage well enough to be able to enjoy myself. I cope with most of the slopes by now when I go with my old mate Wil yr Hafod.

That first programme filmed on the piste was quite special. I had never before been on skis and I ended up on my back more than I stayed on my own two feet. I must have looked exactly like a cow suffering from the milk disease. And it happened during a period when the snow was rather thin on the ground. My tutor was a local man, Pierino, one heck of a character. "Oh, for Christ-a-sake-a, what-a is a-the matter with you?" That was his constant cry. And if things really went haywire he would shout, 'Oh, sheet-a-breeck!'

One of the greatest attractions of working on *Cefn Gwlad* was the variety of language and dialect. I found this especially attractive while working with the Cae'r Berllan brothers, William and Richard. They had a richness of

141

talents and also a richness of language. William was a shire-horse man through and through. And we filmed him shoeing the mare on what was an extremely hot summer's day. It was so hot that the cameraman fainted out in the field.

'Would you like some buttermilk?' asked William.

I was almost dying of thirst, yet I hated buttermilk.

'No, thank you William. I can't drink it. I hate the stuff.'

'Well, well, you should drink it, Dafydd *bech*. It's good for you.'

Just to please him I accepted. 'All right, but just one glassful, William.'

And there I was standing in the corner of the stable under the hot lights watching William shoeing the mare when Maud, William's wife, came in with a glass of buttermilk.

'There we are, Dafydd,' she said. 'A little buttermilk for you.'

I didn't want to embarrass her so I drank it down in one. I don't think it even touched the side, which was an advantage. That way I couldn't taste it much.

'Thank you,' I said.

But I didn't get off so easily. Maude took away the empty glass and returned with a refill. And I had to drink that down as well. Then I had to rush out. I spewed like a cat that had choked on an old milk separator filter. I was sick for the rest of the day.

Such things happened regularly while filming *Cefn Gwlad*. I filmed a series in Snowdonia, which meant climbing, abseiling and rescuing. The worst nightmare of all was climbing Tryfan. I'll never forget that experience for as long as I live. I was working my way round the peak when I happened to look down towards the Bethesda road. A bus was going by. It looked like a Dinky toy. And when a plane

142

flew past I could look directly in through the cockpit window. Looking back, I'm glad that I did it. But at the time, like Pierino, it was 'Sheet-a-breeck.'

I have always been scared of heights, and while climbing Tryfan I broke the sacred rule of all climbers, I looked down. I remember someone once describing danger as playing marbles on eternity's pavement. On Tryfan I knew that beneath me was that very pavement, and nothing else.

Following the televising of that particular episode I remember someone telling me, 'You must have filled your trousers.' But I said no, I didn't. How could I? The ropes were so tight around me there was no room for anything to fill my trousers.

Many of these exploits I would never undertake again. But that was the strength of so many of our programmes. Sometimes it would be too rainy to film certain rural activities. So we would have to change our plans at the drop of a hat. Then we would wonder, 'What can we do instead?' And someone would suggest, 'What about Eric Jones? He'll be out on some crag somewhere. Let's go and see Eric.'

Eric is a world-renowned climber and adventurer who doesn't know the meaning of fear. Some of the feats he has attempted makes me wonder sometimes if he is stark-raving bonkers. Yet he is unbelievably calm and collected and is the nicest man you could ever imagine.

Eric would often be a standby. And that's how many of our programmes were conceived – impromptu and completely unplanned. And again that was an advantage. I would return home from a climbing shoot, or something else just as dangerous, and vow never to do it again. Yet, had I known in advance of some of the tasks that awaited me I would not have left the house that morning.

As a result of all this I have climbed Tryfan and Bwlch Moch. I've paddled a canoe on Llyn Gwynant. Yes, canoeing again. That was another nightmare. The experience of sitting in a canoe was like squatting on an egg-shell. Never again! Well, at least not until the next time.

I was crazy enough once to ride a jet-ski in Cardigan harbour. Behind me on the pillion was a water-bailiff, Caradog Jones. It was exactly like being on a motorbike. I started out well enough but a motor boat swept past us and we were caught in its wake. And down we went. And there I was, scared stiff and bouncing up and down in the water like a cork. Caradog was shouting his advice to me, 'Remember two things, Dai. Don't panic and try to swallow as little water as possible.'

And what comfort his advice brought me! There I was bobbing up and down and spitting out water like a village pump. Luckily a rescue boat came over and picked us up. No, water and I don't mix at all.

For one thing, I can't swim. And that put me in a very awkward situation when I was filming in Cwm Gwaun in Pembrokeshire with some local school children. They were all around eight years old and I was the only one among them that couldn't swim. I had to face the embarrassment of wearing arm-bands and the kids mocked me mercilessly.

My most terrifying experience must have been a special we made on mountain rescue, *Achub Dai* (Rescuing Dai). Usually the rescuers would use a dummy for their exercise, but this time I was the dummy. One manoeuvre involved me being strapped to a stretcher hoisted by a sling and lowered down a cliff face. There I was swinging like a pendulum. I could see Pwllheli in the distance, then Dolgellau, then Pwllheli, then Dolgellau. It was a nightmare.

Cefn Gwlad has unearthed many a character that had never been given the chance of being on television before. One of these was Johnny Moch (Johnny Pigs) from Anglesey. He didn't possess a television set and he didn't know me from Adam. I explained to him that we would like to film him as people like him were few and far between. He eventually agreed and sealed that agreement by pouring me a large measure of whisky into an unwashed cup that he picked up off the table. We spent a week with him, and after finishing the shoot he took me to one side and told me he had a present for me to remember him by. It turned out to be a pair of Doctor Marten boots. He was forever buying goods from travelling salesmen and that's how he had bought the boots. And I still have them.

One of the most memorable programmes was the one we shot with Esmor Evans, the veterinary surgeon from Mold and Betws Gwerful Goch, who also kept a Charolais herd. I was amazed at the high standard of his herd. They were undoubtedly the best Charolais I had ever seen. I suggested to Geraint not to end the programme at the farm, but to accompany Esmor to the Perth cattle show in Scotland. He intended taking around 20 of his best bulls up there to compete. I had a feeling that he would create a little bit of history there.

Geraint agreed and we followed Esmor and his bulls up there. In all, the animals were to compete in five different classes. They won five red cards and numerous blue and yellow cards as well. His bulls made a clean sweep by winning all three of the championship sections they entered. And his champion of champions was sold there for a record price. And I felt proud that our cameras were there to capture all that.

145

I was there with Esmor in the box as the bull was being sold and I found it difficult to decide whether I was at the Perth Show or in Heaven. It was astounding, the bull being sold for a world-record price of 56,000 guineas.

Another programme that will remain for a long time in my memory was the one we filmed with two Llanwrtyd Wells brothers, Jac and Dai Arthur. They were brilliant. Every lunch-break, Jac would demand to come with me down to the Neuadd Arms for dinner. And his tipple would always be a half of mild followed by a glass of port.

Every morning I had to take him a packet of twenty cigarettes. He was a heavy smoker, but only when cigarettes were given to him. So, it was twenty Gold Leaf every morning – at my expense. I had just bought a new car and Jac was admiring it as I drove him to the pub.

'Damn, you've got a nice car, Jones,' he said. 'And what big ashtrays you have.' Yet he would flick the ash on the floor and stub his cigarette out on the dashboard before tossing the stump into the receptacle that held my gloves at the bottom of the passenger door.

I had a sun roof and as we returned one hot day I had opened it. But Jac must have thought that I had opened the passenger-side window. The car had electric windows and hearing Jac clearing his throat I thought I'd better open his window just in case. As soon as I did so he spat out through it.

'Lucky the window was open, Jac,' I commented.

'Oh, Jones *bach*,' said Jac, 'I knew it was open. I could feel the draught.'

The draught, of course, came from the open sun-roof. And there and then I thanked God for electric windows.

Llanwrtyd is renowned for its small farmsteads, many of them having diversified by offering trekking facilities. This has attracted many visitors from England, among them some fashionable young girls, daughters of professional people from the home counties. They would often be targeted by the young men of the area. And not only young men. Jack once took one of them for a walk over the mountains. On the way over, he offered her an orange. She, rather haughtily said, 'No thanks. Oranges are for pregnant women.' Completely unperturbed, Jack answered, 'That's all right, love. You can eat it on the way back.'

The title of the programme was *Jac a Blodwen yr Hwch* (Jac and Blodwen the Sow). He was always longing for the old days when he used to buy pigs for fattening. So we had this idea of buying him a piglet and filming it as it grew. Not only did HTV pay for the piglet, the company also paid for all its food. Occasionally a call would come from the Neaudd Arms. The landlady would do the dialling. Jac didn't know how. Then, having been connected, he would take over the receiver.

'Jones, is that you? Well listen now, the sow's food has run out. Send me a cheque, Jones, will you? About £30 will do. That will pay for everything.'

In about another month he would ring for another cheque. But in the meantime Blodwen grew and grew and the time came for us to take her on her final journey. Jac rang and told us that the sow was ready for slaughtering.

'She's a beautiful pig, Jones. A beautiful pig. But she'll look even more beautiful hanging under the ceiling.'

We had to travel down to Brecon for the slaughter. And the slaughterer told us that he had killed bullocks that were smaller than Blodwen. At dead weight she was 580 lbs. It took all day to load the meat in order to take it back for salting. That was a truly memorable programme.

Children from all over Wales had taken to Blodwen. But she ended her days on Jac's frying-pan. Jac retired soon after that and bought a house that had belonged to a bank manager in Llanwrtyd. And there he lived out his days like a king.

Two members of the same family, this time a brother and sister, were the subjects of another programme in the series. Catrin and Huw Pugh lived in Cwm Ffernol in Pennal. She was a spinster and he a bachelor and they farmed in the old-fashioned way. They had names for all their sheep. There was Gwenno, Beti Wyn, Siân Elin and so on. They also named the cows. One was called Noella, another was Beauty Noella. They did not own a television set and, as in the case of Johnny Moch, they didn't know me, but they did consent to being filmed.

Catrin produced butter in a churn in the traditional way and did all the milking by hand. The crew had arranged to meet at the Riverside in Pennal. The sound-man was late arriving and apologized. 'Don't worry about it,' I said. 'But you'll have to be quick as Miss Pugh is keen to have a game of squash later on this afternoon.' When he saw the place he soon realized that I had been pulling his leg. The only squash Catrin knew anything about was the orange stuff that came in a bottle.

We would encounter a few problems now and again. And at Cwm Ffernol the cows were not used to lights in the cow-shed so we had to install the lamps the night before in the hope that they would get used to them. Catrin had warned us that if the cows became restless we would have to abandon the shoot. It needed more technical skill to film Catrin and Huw's cows than it took to shoot a James Bond film.

I smoked a pipe at that time. But I was ordered to leave my pipe, and the others their cigarettes, on the kitchen table. There was to be no smoking at Cwm Ffernol. I accepted the situation but the sound-man, who was a heavy smoker, would disappear down the lane now and then for a sly drag.

All week I referred to the sister as Miss Pugh. And the last shot of all meant accompanying her in the car. We had opened the shooting with Huw driving the old car, which broke down. But in the meantime they had bought a new Austin Princess, so the ending would show Miss Pugh driving the new car. There she was going through the gears wearing her best red hat. And there was I keeping a vigilant eye as she reversed.

'Fine, Miss Pugh,' I said. 'But don't go any further or you'll hit the garage.'

And to our great amusement she turned to me and said, 'Oh, you can call me Catherine from now on.'

Yes, I had been allowed into Miss Pugh's world.

The programme we shot based on Don Garreg Ddu was also an important milestone in the history of *Cefn Gwlad*. We filmed Don together with his family, especially the two sons, Dico and Bando. Their real names were David, or Dei, and Richard. Referring to Richard as Dico is quite natural, I suppose. But Dei is known as Bando because he goes on and on non-stop like a brass band. He's a very popular lad in the area.

While filming at Garreg Ddu we encountered a problem. We needed to catch the stallion, a blue roan that had never been tethered. But Don didn't foresee any difficulties.

'Well,' said Geraint, who couldn't tell the difference between a stallion and a tomcat, 'leave it be until we arrive.'

And that's what happened. We took the camera up

Garreg Ddu mountain and drove the stallion down to the farmyard. Unfortunately some of the farm out-houses were rather ancient and had been built well before Don's day. We managed to trap the stallion in a shed. But up he reared on his hind legs and the next minute his head was out through the roof. He was kicking and snorting, you could have sworn that a pack of wolves had been cornered in the shed. We did, ultimately, manage to bridle him and for the next two nights I tried to calm him down so we could film him. And I began to gain his confidence. He even allowed me to lead him around the farmyard on a tether.

Now it was time to try and persuade him to take to the traces. His reply was rather emphatic. He kicked a yellow plastic bucket so high that I think it's still up there somewhere in space. But he gradually calmed down and we felt, at last, that we would be able to film him the following morning.

We planned for Don, his two sons and me to walk the stallion down to the field and tether him to a stake. Off we went. But the stallion was rather nervous. Even a sparrow flying from a bush would get him going. Then, suddenly, a startled rabbit sprang in front of us and the stallion took off. His hooves found some firm ground and there was no stopping him. I had been holding on to the end of the rope. But what with the stallion taking off and turning sharply at the same time I found myself up to my knees in a ditch. Eventually we rounded him up and tethered him to a stake. It proved to be quite an adventure.

That wasn't the only adventure at Garreg Ddu. On the night of Bando's birthday some of his friends, unknown to him, had hired a Kissogram girl to come to the party at the Three Crowns at Llanrhaeadr-ym-Mochnant. There had been some trouble between the Garreg Ddu family and some incomers who had settled nearby. They were unhappy with the barking of the dogs and had taken their complaint to the police. So when the Kissogram girl arrived wearing a police uniform and asking for David Morris, Bando assumed that she had come to talk to him about the dogs. And there was quite a discussion between them.

All his friends were chuckling in the background when the girl suddenly stripped off down to her undies. And there was Bando trying to cover her up and telling her not to be so foolish, as she could lose her job in the police force. He still thought that she was a real policewoman. The next day Bando was going round telling everyone how his friends had hired – not a strippogram but a radiogram – for his birthday. Incredible!

We once filmed the poet Gerallt Lloyd Owen at Sarnau. One of his hobbies is shooting clay pigeons and of course, we simply had to get him to teach me. Gerallt had bought a new trap to launch the clays and as it was new its spring was rather strong. In addition to this his clays were old. And having been kept in the boot of his car for some length of time they were rather brittle as well.

I was the first to shoot with Gerallt pulling the lever. But most of the clays shattered of their own volition. And I asked Gerallt for the proper term to describe that sort of incident?

'Oh,' said Gerallt, crossing my line of fire, 'we call that a "no bird".'

'Damn it,' I said, 'if you don't get out of my way it will be no bard.'

Another feather in our cap was the decision to buy a Welsh Black bullock and fatten it for showing at Smithfield.

It was bought from John Hughes, Hafod Ifan, Ysbyty Ifan. And the bullock went on to win the Queen's Cup, every exhibitor's dream at Smithfield. The cup was presented to me by the Queen Mother. And she naturally asked me where I was from? I told her I was from Llanilar. She had never heard of the place. Then I told her it was near Aberystwyth.

'Oh, I've been there many times,' she said. 'The sea looks nice there.'

'Yes,' I agreed. 'But the land looks better than the sea. When you're down there next you'll have to call for a cup of tea.'

She smiled and she promised she would. But she never did.

I experienced an even stranger encounter with Royalty at the Royal Welsh Show. I was one of the announcers in the main ring, sharing shifts with Charles Arch. Charles and I, thanks to the perseverance of the late Llew Phillips, were the first ever to commentate in Welsh from the main ring.

That particular year the chief guest was to be Princess Anne, who was married to Captain Mark Phillips at the time. Various dignitaries had already been chosen to welcome her. Usually, during a Royal visit, you will see the VIPs in their bowler hats surrounding Royalty for the Royal Luncheon. And that year, things were no different. This left just Charles and myself to do the commentating over the dinner-hour. We had to make do with *cawl* and beef slices.

The commentator who should have officially welcomed the Princess had left, and had delegated his duties to Charles. But Charles was cunning enough to make his excuses and leave for the Gents. In the meantime the Princess arrived early and I was left to welcome her to

Llanelwedd. I prattled on for a while in the hope that Charles would shortly return. I postponed the greeting for as long as I could. The reason for this, incredibly, was that I had completely forgotten the Princess's name. I just couldn't recall it. And the longer I dithered the worse it got. I was now praying for Charles to return and save my skin. But to no avail.

On and on I chattered, and having run out of empty words I asked everyone to welcome Mrs Phillips. That story made the papers the following day. Much was made of the fact that a television presenter had referred to Princess Anne as plain Mrs Phillips. She did not complain. But I have a feeling that the bowler-hatted dignitary that accompanied her must have swallowed his shooting-stick.

One who worked with me on many occasions on *Cefn Gwlad* was the late Dewi Bebb, who had won some 35 rugby caps for Wales and also played for the British Lions. He was one of the nicest and kindest persons I have ever met. He loved working on *Cefn Gwlad*, it always made him laugh. He couldn't believe all the fun we had with the various characters.

One programme I filmed with Dewi involved a family from Twll-y-Gwyddyl between Ammanford and Clydach, the Jacobs family. The old lady was 93 years old and while I was interviewing her and her son Islwyn, Dewi couldn't contain his laughter. He would often say that meeting people such as these gave him the same thrill as winning a rugby cap for Wales and running out on the Arms Park.

I'm often asked how we manage to find so many characters and stories for our filming. Well, it has meant some extensive travelling from the very beginning. Geraint lives up north while I live near Llanilar. We would therefore arrange to meet in a certain area and work it much the same way as the old American insurance companies sold their products. We would milk the various areas for stories. Animal fodder reps would be ideal contacts, as would the local minister or vicar. Petrol station attendants and shopkeepers would impart a store of local knowledge. But the best contact of all is the local postman. Postmen know everything there is to know about their localities.

Gradually we built up a network of contacts who would feed us with stories, some of them bordering on the bizarre. We filmed one couple who had pigeons perched on their grandfather clock, and who were on such good terms with the rats that infested their farm that they named them individually.

There have only been a few occasions when I have been unable to persuade someone to appear on *Cefn Gwlad*. One of those rarities was Gwilym Brynllefrith. I had long begged Gwilym to appear on the programme, but his sister would have nothing to do with the idea. She told her brother, 'Gwilym, however much you will be offered to appear on that programme, I will give you double the fee if you don't appear.'

One day I called with Gwilym to ask the way to the home of a possible subject for the show, a man known as Jac Y Wyddor. It was the name of his farm that first attracted me to Jac. *Y Wyddor*, in Welsh, means The Alphabet. Asking the way to Y Wyddor near Trawsfynydd was not my only reason to call with Gwilym. I was secretly hoping that he would relent and allow me to film him. And he was a character well worth filming. He once decided to concrete part of his yard. He went about it in quite a novel way. Firstly he spread gravel over the area that was to be

154

concreted. Then he spread a covering of cement over the gravel, just as if he was spreading lime or guano. He then sprinkled water over it all and used a garden *Rotovator* to mix the lot. Then, as the finishing touch, he used a heavy roller to level it.

Anyway, Gwilym directed me to Jac Y Wyddor. And what a character. Jac bred pigs for the Mold sales. He would store the oatmeal for the pigs in the parlour because his shed was infested with mice. He would often use a horse and cart, and we filmed him taking the mare to be serviced at Garreg Ddu. What a pantomime.

He once borrowed Gwilym Brynllefrith's trailer to ferry his pigs to market. But an official from the RSPCA took him to task because the trailer did not allow enough air to circulate. Jac's response was to grab a drill and bit. The trailer ended up looking like a sieve. On returning the trailer, Gwilym's response was, 'If there wasn't enough air there before, there's enough there now for the pigs to catch pneumonia.'

Jac once advertised his grand piano for sale. There was an immediate response. The potential buyer travelled down the very next day to find Jac feeding the pigs. Jac took him to see the grand piano. His visitor was rather perplexed to find an upright piano.

'Yes, it's an upright piano, all right,' conceded Jac. 'But you must admit, it's a grand one.'

I once sold him a sheepdog. Some farmers use a prefix when naming a dog. For instance, should the dog come from the Rheidol Valley it might be named Rheidol Ben. Jac named his dog Coch Y Wyddor, or The Wyddor Red.

The funniest story regarding Jac happened after a married local man of the cloth had been involved in sexual misdemeanours with another woman. He became involved in a fracas and had assaulted his wife. The scandal even reached the pages of the *Sun* newspaper.

The following day, Jac was drinking in his local when he was accosted by an American visitor who began to boast of his country's achievements while belittling Wales. Jac took the man to task by telling him that Wales would beat America in anything and everything.

'What do you mean?' retorted the man. Wales better than the USA! Why, we've had a man on the moon!'

'That's nothing,' answered Jac. 'Only yesterday we had a vicar in the Sun!'

Having spent 17 years on *Siôn a Siân,* I have now spent over 20 years with *Cefn Gwlad.* And for the past 15 years I have been given the status of co-producer with Geraint Rees. And Marian Hughes, the production assistant, has been with us now for ten years. *Cefn Gwlad*, therefore, is produced by a team of three. And team-work is all-important for the programme's success. We discuss everything together; we understand each other's thoughts and needs. And yet we are able, individually, to organize everything for the common good when we are apart.

Many subjects that have appeared on *Cefn Gwlad* are people I have discovered by visiting agricultural shows and sheepdog trials throughout Wales and beyond. And this again has proved to be a welcomed coincidence for me. For years I frequented eisteddfodau before turning to concert appearances. Then came shows and sheepdog trials. And through them all I have continually turned within rural circles.

Geraint has his roots in Rhuthun, near the heartland of Dyffryn Clwyd and he instinctively knows the likes and dislikes of country people. Marian is from Saron, Denbigh and is herself a farm girl who still travels home regularly from Cardiff to help out on the land. Her roots are deep in the agricultural soil. All three of us, therefore, share the same interests and we contribute equally to the series. We are links in a chain and should one link break, we would find it very difficult. We are so close that not one of us is ever greeted as an individual.

'Hello, Dai, how are Geraint and Marian?' Hello, Geraint, how are Dai and Marian. How are you, Marian, how are Dai and Geraint?'

That is the way of things. And we often receive Christmas cards from people addressed to all three of us. There is a familiarity about us, a familiarity that is not only felt between the three of us, but also between us and our audience.

And if the audience is happy, then we are happy.

10

All my Trials

What with farming and regular television work you might think that I would have no time for anything else. It's true that I don't have as much spare time as I would like, but when I do, I spend it with my sheepdogs.

This is an interest that has been with me since childhood. I well remember my first sheepdog, given to me by John Henry Jones, Llanrhystud, a genius when it came to training dogs. He worked as a shepherd with another great character, Jim Ystrad Teilo and also at Pengarreg. And it was John who brought me my first dog, having registered it first. The dog's name was Prince and I would often take him with me to help round up Dai Morris Jones's sheep on Mynydd Bach and Banc Camddwr.

Dai's annual shearing day at Pantamlwg was quite an occasion. The farm bordered the mountain, so this was a mountain shearing in the true sense of the term. Dai owned three dogs, Panda, Carlo and Cymro and he could make them do anything. Had he wished, I believe Dai could have taught them to knit. As a child I would be spellbound watching Dai's dogs going through their amazing repertoire. And I did my best, of course, to emulate Dai.

Dai owned a tin whistle which had five different notes. Such whistles were rare and would have to be ordered specially from Ted Sewell's shop in Tregaron. Ted was the local saddler, and what a shop. It was an Aladdin's Cave full of collars and leads and whistles and all kinds of paraphernalia. It was a dark little place in Chapel Street and the smell of leather permeated the whole place.

But my first whistle did not come from any shop. It was a hazel-stick whistle whittled by a character from Pontrhydfendigaid, Dai Williams, or Dai Cornwal as he was known. Having fashioned the whistle he tied a piece of string around its end in case I swallowed it.

But to return to Dai Morris. Not only was he an expert with sheepdogs he was also a hunter, and a great man with a gun. He looked the complete sportsman dressed in breeches and leggings. One day, Ianto Rowlands the butcher took his Labrador dog to Pantamlwg to show it off to Dai. He wanted to demonstrate to Dai how good the Labrador was as a gun dog.

'Throw something into the pool there and we'll see what he's like,' said Dai.

Ianto threw a stick into the pool and shouted 'Fetch!' But the dog never moved a muscle.

'Damn it all,' said Ianto, 'what will I do with him?'

'Take him home,' said Dai, 'and throw the stick into his milk bowl. Perhaps then he'll dive in after it.'

I would go to the various sheepdog trials with Will Baigent, Ty Cam and D.C. Morgan, Yr Esgair. And D.C., who was a butcher, was responsible for instilling in me a deep interest in training sheepdogs. He was himself a fervent competitor and I admired him greatly.

The tradition remains in the family through his son, Idris and his own son, Eirian, or Butch who, like his grandfather, is a butcher. And Butch's son took up the hobby when he was still in primary school. I have been a friend of the family from my boyhood. They are the salt of the earth.

Sheepdogs play a very important part in my life. Filming or performing on stage tends to create tension within me. It coils the spring, as it were. And no matter what anyone says, without that tension you don't give of your best. But the dogs help me unwind when I return home.

I attended the very first international sheepdog trial when it was held in Cardiff back in 1959. And as it happened, Wales did very well there. I was given a lift there by the late John Henry Jones and Trefor Evans, Penlan, Llaningel. He too has left us by now. I was only a youngster of 14 or 15 back then. It was in that September just after I left school.

The championship was held on the Ely racecourse. And down I went with Trefor in John Henry's huge Austin 16. With us in the car we carried 15 gallons of water and two dozen eggs. The radiator was leaking and the answer to a leak in those days was to crack an egg and drop it in the radiator. It took us 15 hours to reach Cardiff, an hour for every gallon of water. We had to stop regularly to top up with water and eggs. Trefor just sat there grinning. And by the time we reached our destination we had used up all the eggs.

Having reached Cardiff, John Henry stopped in the city centre to ask for directions to our lodgings. His car differed from today's cars. His car doors opened backwards. They could have proved to be excellent emergency brakes. You only had to open the car doors and the wind would hold it up.

'Where shall we park?' asked John Henry.

'Damn it,' I said, 'park it as far as you can from the other cars. Having swallowed two-dozen eggs it will be feeling a bit randy by now.'

On the Saturday morning just before the final we called in a grocer's shop to buy more eggs. And we filled the radiator with water and some eggs ready for our departure in the morning. But despite all our precautions we got lost on the way. By the time we reached Llandovery a heavy fog had descended. And poor John Henry had no inkling where we were. And as John Henry was lost, so was I. We had absolutely no idea of our bearings.

Gradually we caught up with a car sporting an EJ prefix on its registration plates. And for us to have caught up with it, the driver must have been a slower driver than John Henry. And that is saying something.

'Great,' said John Henry. 'with that number it must be a Cardiganshire car. It must, at least, be heading for Lampeter. We'll follow it.'

And follow it we did. And John Henry made such a good job of following it that we ended up parked right behind it in the driver's garage. He was trembling like a leaf, poor man, when he saw this huge car parked behind him. He must have feared that he had been stalked by three highwaymen. But we were lucky. The man lived in Llanwrda and it was just a short journey from there to Lampeter and home.

The winner in the international championship, by the way, was Meirion Jones of Pwll-glas, Rhuthun with his dog Ben. Ivor Hatfield, a coalman from Prestatyn won the doubles while Bill Miles, Treharris won the prize for driving sheep. The interest in sheepdog trials must have been with me even back then or I wouldn't be able to remember the visit so well.

I gradually started to attend meetings regularly and began competing with Prince. The old dog became a good friend who followed me faithfully for years. I made the acquaintance of some of the stalwarts of the sport, John

Evans from Magor; Herbert Worthington from Abergavenny, Thomas Bryn-mawr, Dai Daniels, Ystradgynlais and his son, Eirwyn, and Cornelius from Ogmore. They would all attend the local trials, including the one at Llangwrddon. From the north would come John Jones, Trawsfynydd, and Alan Jones, as well as Selwyn Jones. I could name dozens of them.

My interest in the eisteddfod circuit had led to a comparatively long absence from competing in sheepdog trials. Then, following my successes in the two Blue Ribbon events I felt I needed a hobby. So I reverted to my interest in sheepdogs. I bought a young bitch from Olwen's uncle, Ocky Davies from Brecon. He was a Tregaron man and the bitch's name was called Jill. And she rekindled my interest.

I was then given a young bitch, Meg, by Alan Jones as payment for appearing in a concert. And gradually I began spreading my wings and competed further afield.

One of the first meetings I attended following my renewed interest was held at Caerwedros. The local sports-meeting was held on the same evening. Quite a substantial crowd had gathered and the announcer informed over the tannoy that I would be the next competitor.

'Next we have Dai Jones,' he said. 'You all know him as the presenter of *Siôn a Siân* and as one who has entertained audiences throughout Wales.'

That did it. All the crowd from the sports meeting joined those watching the trials. And that made me feel nervous. Facing 300 people as an audience in a concert hall doesn't bother me one bit. But with the same number behind me at a sheepdog trial I'll be shaking like a leaf. And this meeting at Caerwedros was no exception. I don't know why this should be. It could be the fact that I have to depend so much on the dog.

On that occasion my dog was Moss. I had bought him from Alan Jones for £650. He was a large black dog and he wasn't performing as well as I would have liked. He was rather undependable. But now I had a large audience who was expecting something big from Moss and me.

I took him to the starting post and set him off. But instead of fetching the sheep he leapt through the judge's car window and scattered his papers like confetti. The judge started shouting and this frightened Moss who proceeded to pee over the man's spectacles. I hadn't seen anything like it in my life. Neither had the audience. They were falling about laughing. Had I paid them a thousand pounds and told them the best joke ever thought of they wouldn't have laughed more.

Eventually I did manage to send Moss away. But only after he had finished peeing. He made a good run but failed to win a prize. The old dog had stained his character – and the judge's papers and spectacles – before he had even started.

The friends you make in the sheepdog fraternity tend to be, like the dogs themselves, a breed of their own. And I treasure their company. For well over a quarter of a century I have been elected one of 15 directors of the Sheepdog Society. I have served several terms on the Council and have achieved the honour of having been the Welsh President. Each of the home countries has its own President who serves for four years, and I am proud to have represented Wales.

During the second year of my presidency I found things very difficult. I was asked to pay tribute at the gravesides of several stalwarts of the society. And like any other society, it has occasionally suffered its own internal problems. Having said that, I have found it a pleasure to serve as President.

I still run dogs and I visit the International Trials every year. It was wonderful for me when the trials came to the Towy valley.

But the enjoyment, from first to last, is created by the people themselves. Many of them by now have left us. And I feel their loss greatly. And here I must refer once again to D.C. Morgan. I remember cycling over to Esgair to see him. And there was D.C. demonstrating to me how to handle the dog. Then, as I mounted the bike and started for home he warned me that I should always keep the dog between me and the hedge.

'What?' I asked, 'All the way home?'

'Yes, every step of the way. If he tries to make for your outside, stop him and return him to your inside. That's where he should be.'

Yes, D.C. was quite the master.

One of the pleasures of the sheepdog world was the occasional trip up to Scotland to take a bitch to be mated by one of the top dogs. And Scotland can boast many such dogs. One of those visits will live forever in my memory. And here D.C. Morgan's grandson, Butch, played a big part. Butch has a rather squeaky voice but he is a very determined character where dogs are concerned. He rang me one Friday night.

'What are you doing tomorrow?' he asked.

'Nothing much. Why do you ask?'

'I'm taking the bitch up to Scotland. Fancy a trip?'

I agreed immediately.

'I will be closing the shop around 3.30,' he said. 'Then we'll go.'

Butch owned a rather large car, a Rover V8 Vitesse. It was quite a car. We put the bitch in the boot and off we went around four o' clock in the afternoon. We drove non-stop to Charnock Richard where we called in for a meal. He was going on about the need for new sparking plugs and new points for the car. To him it seemed sluggish. To me it was going fast enough as Butch was hitting the hundred mark quite often. But it wasn't fast enough for him.

The bitch was called Phil. She hadn't done one day's work in her life. But Butch had bought her because she was of good breeding stock. He hoped he could breed good off-spring from her. And indeed, he did just that. But as a trial runner she was useless. She was more of a pet than a working bitch.

We left Charnock Richard at dusk and I warned Butch to be careful as I had spotted a police car lurking by the side of the motorway, a low-built car that looked fast.

'Don't worry,' said Butch, 'he's stopped.'

'Hell, be careful,' I said, 'don't take a risk.'

Suddenly the car pulled out and started following us. It caught up with us quite easily. And Butch was now caught between two minds. Should he pull over or go hell for leather? I advised him to slow down.

The police car passed us and the driver waved us down. Out of the car came a solitary policeman.

'In a hurry, gentlemen?' he asked."

'Damn, not really,' said Butch. 'She only came on heat last week. They usually last a fortnight.'

The policeman was puzzled. 'What do you mean, heat?'

'Oh, sorry,' said Butch, 'we've got a bitch in the boot and we're taking her up to Scotland to mate her. There's no hurry. She won't go off for another week.'

'The way you're speeding, you'd think she wouldn't last till tomorrow morning.' By now the officer was smiling.

'But the way you passed me back there, you almost blew me out of my car.'

And Butch answered, 'Damn it all, you should always remember to wear your seat-belt.'

The outcome was that the policeman had no option but to book Butch as his speed had been recorded by radar. There I was looking around trying to appear unconcerned while the traffic whizzed by. Butch in the meantime was trying to persuade the officer that other cars passing us were travelling far quicker than he had been.

The officer now had his notebook out and was about to book Butch and he asked for his name. Butch blurted out, 'David Eirian Morgan.'

'Good God!' exclaimed the officer, 'how do you spell that?'

And Butch saw a glimmer of hope.

'Are you sure you want to book me? Because if you have difficulty with my name, you'll never be able to write down my address.'

With my help he managed with Butch's name. Then he asked for his address. And Butch rattled it off.

'Bancllyn, Bontnewydd, Blaenpennal, Tregaron.'

The officer scratched his head in bewilderment. 'My God, you must have a very educated postman in your neck of the woods.'

Butch grabbed the notebook from the officer's hand and wrote the address down on his behalf. By now the policeman had become quite friendly.

'What do you do for a living?' he asked.

And Butch replied, 'I'm a butcher. What do you do?'

The policeman smiled wanly and wished us the best of

luck. And turning to Butch he asked him, 'Should the bitch have puppies, send me a card and let me know.'

Off we went and in the mirror I could see the officer still shaking his head. We aimed for Edinburgh where we were to visit Dick Fortune, the owner of the dog who was to mate with Phil. Dick had spent most of his life in New Zealand and the dog's name was Fortune's Glen. Dick was one of the best dog handlers in the world. He was around 80 years old but was married to a woman almost half his age. And she looked like a model.

Having welcomed us warmly, Dick gave us an instant exhibition on handling sheepdogs. Incidentally, I consequently sold him one of my own bitches, Meg, for £600. He sold it on to an American breeder.

Well, Butch's bitch was serviced and we prepared to leave, intending to spend the night nearer home. But Dick insisted we stayed at his place. And we gladly accepted. Our host told us we could sleep in his room as it had two double beds. He would spend the night with his wife.

'It's up to you,' I said. 'But if you like, I'll sleep with your wife and you can share with Butch.'

Dick laughingly declined the offer but insisted that we should, before turning in, share his hospitality even more. He opened a bottle of whisky. Then we all turned in. Butch's bitch had been locked in the shed. Butch now took off his clothes and jumped into bed. And when we were both ready for a good night's sleep he tugged the light-pull. Unfortunately he pulled as if he was a church bell-ringer and the cord snapped. Butch stood on the bed and removed the cap from the light-pull socket. But he couldn't thread the end of the cord into the eye where it should be secured. So he stuck the end of the cord between his teeth to try and sharpen the end. But as he inserted the end of the thread into the socket he touched a live wire. Of course, he received a sharp shock and he howled.

Dick must have heard him from the next room and he shouted, asking us if we were all right? But we were laughing too much to answer. And I'll never forget the sight. Butch was leaning out of the window and was shaking with laughter. But the funniest part of it was seeing his buttocks trembling as a result of the shock. Butch is a very hairy man and the electric charge had made the hairs on his back quiver. It reminded me of a breeze blowing through the leaves of a gooseberry bush.

Ultimately he succeeded in mending the light-pull. But just as I was about to drop off he started laughing again. I asked him what was so funny?

'Imagine it,' he said, the words coming out between sobs of laughter, 'Out there in the yard are some of Britain's best dogs running free while my bitch, who hasn't even managed a day's work in her life, is locked up in case somebody steals her.'

I swear we didn't sleep a wink all night. We were too busy laughing.

There was another time when we drove up to Scotland. We were heading for Dunoon in Argyleshire. It got too late for us to drive there all the way the same day so we stopped near Lockerbie just off the A73 to try and catch a few hours' sleep. With the bitch in the boot we had to leave the windows open because of the smell.

'Damn it, Butch,' I said, "what would people say if they knew that we were sleeping with a bitch in a lay-by on the A73?"

Butch had a fit of laughter. And when Butch laughs it

isn't at all safe to be anywhere near him. Especially in his butcher's shop. He laughs so uncontrollably and thumps the counter so hard that the knives dance up and down.

We slept well and continued on our journey, reaching the far side of Glasgow by about four o'clock in the morning. We had two hours to spend before the ferry left.

'Damn, we're too early,' said Butch. There was nowhere to go even for a cup of tea, so we slumbered for a while. But the bitch was smelling so strongly that I asked Butch to take her out of the boot. He did and tethered her to the front bumper. Then we both fell asleep. I was the first to wake up. And Butch can be grateful to me for waking up when I did. Through the windscreen I saw a huge black Labrador playing around with the bitch.

I was tempted to let the dog have his way just for devilment. But I thought I had better wake Butch. When he saw the Labrador he tried to jump out of the car. Unfortunately he was still tied up in his safety-belt and he half-fell out. It took me quite a while to free him. And as soon as he was free he started running down the road chasing the randy Labrador and threatening him with every kind of retribution.

Eventually we reached the ferry, and as we were early we headed the queue. Butch had no idea how to board the boat. So I explained to him that the bow doors would open and then he would be able to drive in. As the doors opened, Butch was immediately into gear. Thankfully the stern doors were closed, otherwise he would have driven straight through and into the Clyde.

The ferry had a toilet and wash-room and I took advantage of the facilities to splash some water over my face and shave. The facilities, it's true, were pretty primitive

169

but by looking at my reflection in a metal fitting above the bowl I was able to scrape away most of the stubble.

When I returned, Butch borrowed my razor and soap and took my place. But when he came out, every passenger on the ferry was in stitches. Never in my life have I seen anyone in such a state. You could have sworn that the IRA had detonated a bomb in his breast pocket. Half the toilet roll was now in little bits all over Butch's face. Wherever he had cut himself there was a scrap of bloodied toilet paper. Wherever there wasn't a cut there was thick stubble. In other words, the only areas on his face where there wasn't any paper were the ones where the razor had missed.

'For God's sake, Butch,' I said, 'go back and wash those bits of paper off or people will think you're suffering from the plague.'

Well, we arrived at Dunoon, a beautiful little village with a row of small hotels and B&B's.

'Think how lucky we are,' said Butch, bringing the bitch to such a lovely place.'

In we went to a small hotel to order breakfast. And Butch was able to tidy himself up in a proper bathroom. He finished off what he had started on the ferry. After a belly-full of breakfast we were off to meet Stuart Davidson and his dog, Ben. There we received a great welcome – and another breakfast. My belly was now as tight as a drum.

The dog wasn't home so we had to travel further on along a mountain road that reminded me of the journey from Tregaron to Abergwesyn. It was the kind of road that could easily double as a switch-back ride in Rhyl fun-fair. The weight of two breakfasts and the nature of the road were now beginning to tell – with the bacon chasing the sausages all around my stomach. As we arrived I could feel

Butch, who was sitting in the middle, pushing against me. I leapt out just in time. Butch jumped past me and the contents of his stomach gushed just past my left ear.

That was a journey to remember. We had left Aberystwyth at five o'clock on Saturday evening and we were back by Sunday supper-time, around 9.45. And there was a happy ending. The bitch gave birth to eight pups.

Yes, Butch. In my estimation he is listed among the immortals. He has a head as bald as a Mint Imperial, he has a high voice and he always wears a pair of braces. Even if he wore the most expensive suit from Saville Row, he would also wear braces, usually a red pair. And when I see him wearing them I ask him, in jest, which is the live wire and which is the earth? Even at a funeral, when wearing a black suit, the red braces are a must. It's a kind of post-office red and the straps are as broad as the belts of a chaffing machine. Butch is unique.

One of the most outstanding characters among the sheepdog fraternity was Evan James, or Ianto Henbant. Not only was Ianto a great character, he was also a brilliant competitor. Trials had started at Caer Belan near Caernarfon. It was a big event with three courses being used at the same time on the site of the old airfield. Competitors and supporters had arrived from all parts of Britain and beyond. Ianto's chest was a bit tight and he was leaning on a car, a foreign car. While resting there he was reading the various stickers on the car windows. The owner of the car, a lady from Holland, came over and started making conversation. Ianto, making small talk, asked her the price of petrol in Holland?

'Oh, in the region of one-and-a-half guilders per litre,' she replied.

'Oh, I see,' said Ianto. 'About the same as around here, then.'

I'm sure that Ianto didn't know the difference between a guilder and a litre. But it was a good reply.

Henbant, where Ianto lived, is exactly a mile-and-a-half from my home and one night I took the bitch over with me. It was just before Christmas and I had three duties to perform. I had to call for the turkey at Ffosbompren. I was to collect Olwen's present from Rhodmâd, where the owner of a fashion shop lived. And I was to take the bitch over to Henbant.

I began with the most important task, taking the bitch to mate with Ianto's dog. I left the house around 7.30. On the way I called with a present for Sal in Cilcwm. Which actually made it four duties. In return she gave me a bottle of whisky. When I arrived Ianto said, 'Damn, I haven't had a drink this Christmas. I've been too busy to go out.'

I told him I had a bottle of whisky in the car. He didn't want to go to the house just then. But we didn't have any glasses to drink from. Then Ianto remembered that he had some chemical in the cowshed for killing warble flies. With the container were two plastic cups for mixing the stuff.

'We'll use these,' said Ianto.

When I left, Ianto was sitting in the cows' drinking bowl and the bottle was half-empty. I remembered the turkey but I completely forgot Olwen's present. I had to return for that the following day.

I also remember taking another bitch to one of Henbant's dogs. He was called Lad and he was a really good dog. Everyone knew him. He was almost as great a character as his owner. I had already asked Ianto on the phone whether it was convenient for me to call.

'Come up now. Immediately,' answered Ianto. 'I'll see you straight away.'

I left the house around 8.30 in the morning but I didn't get home till the same time that evening. Ianto was there on his own. He had just returned from a sheepdog trial held in Ireland and had brought with him a large bottle of *Paddy* whiskey.

'Come in,' said Ianto, 'Leave the bitch for a minute and come in. Damn it, have you ever seen a bottle like this before? Damn it all, it's so big you need planning permission to open it.'

And we attacked the bottle. Now, even the smell of *Paddy* whiskey, to quote Ianto, is enough to make you feel at home. And we drank every drop of the one-litre bottle. No food during all that time. Just whisky. I returned home with the bitch which hadn't even left the Land Rover. Back I went with the bitch the following Monday. And Ianto whispered to me a warning not to breathe a word about the whisky. He had, in the meantime, been to town to buy a bottle of *Grouse* and had poured the contents into the *Paddy* bottle. And now, as she poured the tea, Mrs James turned to her husband and told him, 'Ianto, give Dai a drop of that whiskey you brought back from Ireland.'

If she only knew!

And that is why I am in the business of sheepdog trials. It's the characters that appeal to me, people like Alan Jones, Selwyn Jones, Butch and Charles Arch. And when the international trials visited Ceredigion in 1999, Charles was the course director.

Sheepdogs have given me a reason to live. They are my hobby and the only sport, apart from tennis, that appeals to me. Yet the only time I have really felt nervous in front of a camera was at a meeting in Caernarfonshire. It was filmed for television at the time when I was the Welsh captain. I sent the dog away but for some strange reason I forgot his name completely. And everything became one big shambles. Among other misdemeanours he jumped head-first into the river, and managed to soak both cameraman and camera.

One of the best dogs I ever owned was Mal. He was given to me as a present by a good friend, Aled Jarman of Llanbryn-mair. I had been over there filming Mal Edwards, who had been a drover, for *Cefn Gwlad*. And because the dog came from that locality, which was in Maldwyn, the Welsh name for Montgomery, I decided to name him after Mal. He won me many a trophy and was a wonderful farm dog. More than that, he was a friend.

Seven years ago I received a great honour: I was chosen as a member of the Welsh team. This meant that Mal and I represented our nation. That, to me, is a dream realized.

Mal died five years ago. He was 16 years old. I was away in America filming *Rasus* when I was told he was suffering and I gave the vet the go-ahead to put him down. All my other dogs had been buried on my land but Mal was cremated. I still miss him.

When I am away, as I often am, I constantly think of the dogs. When things get tedious, I always turn to them in my mind. They are very close to my heart.

My great sorrow has been the loss of so many good friends from the sheepdog circuit. There are, thank God, a few left. Evans Blaenglowon died not long ago. I was Vice-President when Evans was President and he taught me a lot. I well remember him competing at Ponterwyd, and at 86 years old he was the first to run a dog there. And that was at seven o'clock in the morning. There are, thank God, a few left.

One aspect of sheepdog trials in particular appeals to me – the fact that they are held in every locality in Wales. And they invariably attract certain types. I have never rubbed shoulders with people who can jest and exchange pleasantries in such a way. But they are fast disappearing and there are not many youngsters coming forward to take their place. And during my Presidency, it was a personal sadness for me to say a few words of tribute at their gravesides. It happened in Meirion Jones's funeral. He died during a sheepdog trial. Then there was Bill Miles, Treharris. It's said that Bill managed to buy a farm with the proceeds of the successes of one of his dogs, Wally, back in the 40s. Then there was that lovely man, Eirwyn Daniels, Ystradgynlais. And add to them that great character, Ianto James, Henbant.

But hand in hand with grief comes gratitude and humility from being asked by their families to say a few words of thanks at their gravesides. As someone else once said, we shall never see the likes of them again.

11

Over my Shoulder

In the old days, when a ploughman had finished ploughing, he would stand on the headland at dusk and review his work. He would look back along the furrows and enjoy great satisfaction if he saw that his furrows were straight. In Welsh, this looking back on a day's work *o ben talar*, from the headland, has taken on the meaning of someone reviewing his own life.

Dic Jones, himself a farmer and a fine poet has described this feeling perfectly:

> 'Mine is the pleasure at the close of day
> If my furrow sometimes a fair picture makes,
> And on that day when things go not so well,
> Give me the right to make my own mistakes.

And as I look back over my life – and like everyone else, the older I get the more often I tend to do that – I reflect on those that have enriched it, those that have helped to keep my furrows straight. I have already spoken of my local childhood heroes. But I also have heroes that have trodden a wider stage. And of those, three personalities stand higher than everyone else.

My trinity of heroes are Richard Rees, the singer; Alan Jones, the sheepdog expert, and Elystan Morgan, or Lord

Elystan as he is now known, the former politician who is now a lawyer and a judge.

Richard Rees was probably my very first real hero. I remember seeing him on television when I was a boy. He made such an impression that I can even remember the brand of Wellington boots that he wore as he brushed the yard outside the cowshed. They were Argyll boots. I can still see them clearly.

That was the first time I ever heard him sing *Aros Mae'r Mynyddau Mawr* (The Great Hills Still Stand). And to me, no one in Wales, or even in the world, has ever sung that song like Dic. Brilliant as Bryn Terfel is, wonderful as Sir Geraint Evans was – two singers who have graced the world stage – I challenge anyone to sing it like Dic Rees Pennal. I could add to it two other pieces, *Y Marchog* (The Knight) and *Y Dymestl* (The Tempest). He left his own indelible stamp on these three songs. I swear that Meirion Williams must have composed *Aros Mae* with Dic in mind. The other two songs were, of course, composed much earlier. But you couldn't find anyone that could perform them better than Dic Rees.

Dic was a singer and a farmer, and that's what I was always striving to be. I wanted to be a successful farmer and I wanted to win the Blue Ribbon in the National. After I acheived that second goal at Ammanford, Dic rang me. His words were, 'We have to meet, Deio *bach*.'

I can't say that I had really met him until then. I had heard him sing, of course. But ever since that success at Ammanford, which is 33 years ago by now, not one week would go by without one of us ringing or visiting the other.

One of my greatest experiences, one which I will always treasure, is the album that Dic and I recorded as a duet.

What is more we travelled together all over Wales and much of the world. And the common factor throughout was our mutual interests. When we were together we discussed music and farming almost in the same breath.

Sometimes those two interests would come together in the most unlikely ways. Dic and I were due to appear together for an engagement at Rhes-y-cae. I met Dic at his home and we drove up together in his Rover. But back in Pennal, Dic's wife, Menna, couldn't find the dogs anywhere. So she rang the home of the concert secretary and asked if she could speak to Dic. By now he was dressed in his tail coat and all the trimmings. Dic told Menna to hold on and he went out to check the car. There in the boot were the dogs as happy as larks. Dic had been out rounding up the sheep earlier that morning and had left the dogs in the boot. And there he was in his concert garb trying to cross the road holding on to two lengths of bale twine which were tied to the two dogs' collars so he could tether them while he performed.

Once, over the Saint David's festival, Dic and I toured together for a whole week singing oratorios as guests of various Welsh societies. Towards the end of that tour we sang at Sheffield on a Friday night, Birmingham the following night and then we travelled down to Cardiff on Sunday morning to record items for a television programme, when we sang two solos each and two duets.

Yes, Richard Rees or as I knew him, Dic Rees Pennal. A real hero. And it is a great feeling when your hero is also one of your closest friends.

The second hero, who was also a valued friend, is Alan Jones of Pontllyfni. Once, when I needed a dog to train for the sheepdog trials, I rang Alan to tell him I would like to travel up to see him. My intention was to arrive at his home, Lleuar Bach, the following morning. His first question was, what did I mean by morning? Did I mean ten? Did I mean eleven?

'Damn it,' I said, 'eleven to me is dinner time. I'll be up by half-past-nine.'

And that's exactly what I did. But by the time I arrived he had persuaded Medwen, his wife, to prepare dinner for me. That's the earliest dinner I've ever had. I remember that well. And I can remember that the dog's name was Bill.

Shortly afterwards I visited the area again, this time to sing in a variety concert, or *Noson Lawen*. Alan had helped to organize the event so, as a friend, I refused any payment. But I didn't sing for nothing. Following the concert Alan led me out into the shed and gave me the pick from a litter of sheepdog pups. These were a special breed and I chose a bitch called Meg. And Meg and I competed together for years.

I still run dogs and over the years I was a regular visitor to Lleuar Bach. Coincidentally, Dic lived at Penmaen Bach and Alan at Lleuar Bach. *Bach,* of course, is Welsh for 'small'. But in both homes, the welcome was anything but small. It was always huge. Indeed, both were like home from home to me. Should I be filming up north and within reach of Llanllyfni I would never fail to call with Alan. Sometimes we wouldn't turn in till around two or three o'clock in the morning. Alan tended to reminisce and would turn out every drawer in the dresser in his search for photographs of some of the dogs he used to run all over Britain, including Hyde Park.

Alan was taken very ill some years ago when he was struck down by cancer. He received serious and prolonged treatment. He recovered and looked as if he had been transformed from near-death to a healthy life. And I swear that in Alan we had a man whose life was saved by his undying love for his dogs.

There is a story of a close relative, one of the Pritchard brothers, visiting Alan in hospital. Pritchard was on his way to Brynsiencyn across the Menai Straits to a sheepdog trial. Alan was flat on his back in the Caernarfon and Anglesey Hospital and his visitor was going on about the attributes of the dog he was going to run that day. Suddenly Alan turned to his wife.

'Medwen,' he said, 'go home to fetch Vic, my dog. By God, I'll beat Pritchard and his dog from here.'

That's the sort of man he was. A great leg-puller, a humorous man. He was full of quips and was a huge personality. He was also a huge man who stood around six feet tall. But he was of a kind disposition, one of nature's gentlemen.

Olwen and I were invited to the wedding of his son Wyn. He is Alan and Medwen's only son and is now a barrister. Not only was I a guest, but I sang there as well. In the reception afterwards Alan spotted me at the bar. He himself was a teetotaller.

'Let me buy you a drink, Dai,' he said.

I ordered a shandy for myself and a Coke for Olwen. Alan threw twenty pounds on the table and asked, 'Is that enough?'

That proved to me that he had no idea regarding the price of drinks.

Alan was the complete Welshman and it was worth hearing him speak English. He wasn't always sure of himself if he didn't speak Welsh. But in his own language he was always original and witty. Someone asked him once at a sheepdog trial where could he park. And Alan answered him, 'Listen here, the way your dogs perform try parking with the disabled.'

Once he was on his way up to the Sheepdog Society meeting in Carlisle. With him in the car, slumbering peacefully, was one of his friends, Gwynfor Pritchard. Alan hit the kerb pretty hard and his friend jumped up in fright.

'Take care,' he said, 'or you'll kill us all.'

'Go back to sleep,' said Alan calmly, 'and I'll see to it that you'll go in your dreams.'

After 21 years, the old enemy caught up with Alan. But so determined was he that, despite his last illness, he vowed to compete once more at Glynllifon sheepdog trials close to his home. Not only did he compete, he won. Alan's best dog had been a champion sheepdog called Roy. And to make the circle complete, the dog that won him his last trial was also called Roy.

At Alan's funeral I was asked to be one of the bearers. As I was on my way to Edinburgh, I parked my car some way from the cemetery. Seeing me making my way to the churchyard, the undertaker stopped and invited me to join him in the hearse. And so I accompanied Alan on his last journey.

Now to the third great hero, Elystan Morgan. Why Elystan? I'm far from being a political person but I remember him when he was the MP for the county and I often heard him speak in public. I fell under the spell of his oratory. It was a pleasure to listen to him on the radio or on television arguing his corner. He had – and still has – a mastery of words. And this gift has always fascinated me.

I had heard Uncle Morgan speak of Lloyd George, and to

me this was another politician from the same mould. This admiration had nothing at all to do with party politics. I admired him as a man. And even more importantly, as a Cardi.

Should he appear somewhere as a guest speaker, for instance, as he did in many an agricultural meeting or conference, he would have this ring in his voice, a kind of dramatic lilt. And he was just as accomplished in both languages. He would change from Welsh to English and vice-versa without pausing. And in doing this he seemed to strengthen the point he was trying to make.

When he lost his seat, I just couldn't understand how the constituents could let go of such a man, whatever their party. Should he have stood even for the Cats' Appreciation Party, and fully realizing my hatred of those particular creatures, I would still have voted for him.

I got to know him well, he and his wife Alwen and the children, Owain and Eleri. And I went out canvassing for him when he attempted to regain the seat. And I can honestly say with hand on heart that it was the most enjoyable pursuit that I have ever undertaken. I would travel mostly with Gwynne Hughes Jones, the county's drama organizer, who was Elystan's cousin. And on the morning of polling day I accompanied Elystan to every polling station in the constituency.

I once accompanied Gwynne and Elystan's son, Owain, to Ystumtuen. Anyone who knows north Ceredigion will appreciate how isolated and remote the place is. And there we were, all three of us, touring the area with a loudspeaker. I would do the preaching. But there was hardly anyone to listen to me, apart from sheep. But I even wanted them to realize that Elystan was their man.

As we drove along I spotted a man pottering around in

182

his garden near his cottage by the side of the road. I told Gwynne to stop so that I could chat with the man. When I saw his huge Jaguar parked outside I knew I was on a hiding to nothing. Despite that, out I went and I soon realized that he was an incomer.

In my best Sunday English I asked him whether he was prepared to back Elystan by voting for him the coming Thursday? He had never heard of Elystan. He hardly realized there was a general election pending. I explained to him that Elystan Morgan represented the Labour Party. And by now I was fascinated with the man's accent.

'Oh, the Labour Party,' he said. 'No, I might as well tell you right now that I won't be supporting Labour. You see, it's this bloody nationalizing they're obsessed with. They'll nationalize anything.'

'Well, damn it all,' I said, 'you've got nothing to nationalize up here apart from rabbits and rushes.'

The way he looked at me was enough to let me know that even if he wasn't previously a Labour supporter, he wouldn't be one now.

We had lots of fun in those days. Despite party differences we were all friends. I would get a great thrill from touring the small villages. Once we crossed from Ffair Rhos to Ysbyty Ystwyth, and there I was, bellowing through the loudspeaker.

'Dear friends . . .'

I could hear my voice echoing back along the valley. Some would pause from their gardening to listen. Another would stagger out from his garden privy holding up his trousers having been disturbed. He must have thought that his neighbour had bought a new radio set with a very high volume capacity.

That reminds me of a couple who kept lodgers during the summer. And the old lady, trying to please, knitted a cover for the lavatory seat in the garden privy. Out went her husband one night. But when he sat down he thought he was sitting on someone's lap. Up he jumped, but as he ran out his braces caught on a nail in the door. And there he was in the dark shouting for his wife to help him.

'Mari, come quick, the bugger has grabbed me.'

But to return to that election. I remember travelling to Aberaeron with the Liberal party car ahead of us. They would shout one slogan. We would shout a different message. Through the streets of Aberaeron it became a game of hide-and-seek with one car trying to get ahead of the other.

On one street the Liberals had regained the lead and in passing one particular house, not noticing the Labour posters, they shouted out the Liberal message. As they did so a formidable-looking woman stepped out brandishing a mop. And the canvasser quipped, 'Well, that old bugger isn't supporting us anyway.' Unfortunately he hadn't switched off his loudspeaker and his words echoed all along the street.

We all, whatever party, canvassed in earnest of course in support of our own particular candidate. But when we broke for dinner, all our differences would be forgotten and we would all congregate in the same cafe or fish and chip shop and be good friends.

Elystan lost and was elevated to the House of Lords as Lord Elystan. But I still believe that it was Cardiganshire's biggest loss politically.

I have never been a party animal. When Cynog Dafis stood for Plaid Cymru, I backed him. To me, the candidate

184

is the important factor. Elystan, in my mind, was on the same level as Lloyd George and James Griffiths. And had he not lost Cardiganshire he would, I'm sure, have ended up as a high-ranking Labour Minister.

It is all-important that Welsh electorates elect MPs who are in touch with the people they represent. They should be Members who know their own people, Members who know their own limits.

I still remember some of Elystan's words, especially when he would quote *Brad Dynrafon,* that old eisteddfod favourite, where the pirates light the 'enticing flame' to lure the boat onto the rocks. He saw the Tory Party as the pirates. And some 18 years later he was proved to be right.

We all have our heroes. And I have dozens. But the greatest of these are Dic, Alan and Elystan. Three heroes, three friends. How poignant, therefore, that I should receive my University of Wales Fellowship certificate from Elystan Morgan, the only member of my trinity of heroes now left.

Looking back from the headland again, I can say that I fulfilled a dream when I twice visited *Y Wladfa*, the Welsh settlement in Patagonia. But as I followed the road from Porth Madryn to Trelew and from Trelew to the Gaiman, despite my feeling of fellowship with the Welsh exiles, I soon realized that the land I was crossing was a desert. Only in Esquel did I encounter some life, some hope. I feel sure that some of those founding fathers cursed Michael D. Jones, their instigator, when they saw such wilderness. They must have had tears in their eyes. They probably felt like packing their bags and returning to Wales instantly.

Having said that, I would love to return to shoot more television documentaries on the Welsh descendants that remain there – especially the older generation. I know that more and more Welsh-speaking tutors are sent out there these days to help the youth of Patagonia resurrect the language. But it will never be as vibrant as it is among the old people, with their number dwindling from year to year. We owe them a great debt, not only for keeping the language alive but also for safeguarding our traditions.

The exiles missed Wales so much that they retained anything that could remind them of home. The traditional Welsh tea, for instance. There are more tea houses there than there are bars. And it's a great experience to visit one of those houses and enjoy the traditional Welsh fare of tea, jelly and trifle and the bread-and-butter with a choice of two or three jams. And, of course, the cakes.

Yes, I'm glad to have been there. But I know that I would not have enjoyed being one of those Pilgrim Fathers who settled there almost 150 years ago. And I have this idea at the back of my mind. Most of the Patagonian-Welsh dream of being able to visit Wales. I would like the Welsh Assembly to consider paying for every Welsh Patagonian who is over 65 years old to come over to visit the Royal Welsh Show and the National Eisteddfod. It wouldn't involve much expense but it would be such a nice way to say 'Thank you'.

In the meantime I don't intend changing my way of life greatly. I'm pleased to say that my television work has kept me busy well into the new Millennium. I can only pray that my health will permit me to continue. I have no great urge to do anything different. I have had the pleasure and the honour of coexisting with the inhabitants of rural Wales. And that is why I shall never leave the heartland. And that also is why I must dedicate this simple volume of reminiscences to the people of Wales for accepting me, and for giving me such a chance in life.

One task I always avoid is opening the mail. I have no idea how many bills arrive at Berthlwyd. Likewise I have no idea how many cheques arrive. All I can hope is that the cheques outnumber the bills.

Money, as such – if I have completed any task to my satisfaction – does not particularly worry me. I never carry a cheque-book. But I'm a great believer in the hole-in-the-wall. I use that regularly even though I have occasionally lost my banker's card. No, after a satisfactory day's work I turn to my sheepdogs for relaxation.

As far as television work goes I would wish to broaden somewhat and film more exiles from rural Wales who have settled abroad. It would be interesting to compare their way of life to that of the ones that have remained in Wales. And in years to come I will enjoy seeing how some of the young people whom I filmed as children have fared.

I have now appeared on television without a break since 1969, which amounts to 35 years. And that is a long enough period in anyone's life, in any kind of work.

Today I keep a herd of Welsh Black cattle. That is still my main occupation. I also keep a flock of some 1,000 ewes, a mixture of Half-breeds and Welsh sheep. I still love farming, the feeling of the soil underneath my feet. And I haven't regretted anything. Not even turning down that chance to study opera in Italy.

I have been privileged to mix with wonderful people and I have been blessed with true friends. The people of Wales have been kind to me, or *clên* to me, as the people of Montgomeryshire would say. And I do love the Montgomery accent. Were I not a Cardi and God raised me high in the sky and told me to choose my favourite spot on earth I would plump for Maldwyn. I love the county and its people.

A good example of the inhabitants of that lovely county is Don Garreg Ddu. He is a blue-print of what every Welshman should be. Today the only factor that counts in the farming world is to take over a farm and make it pay a certain amount per acre. We have followed that philosophy for too long. To the older generation, raising a family and safeguarding the inheritance came before profit. I believe that we should put more emphasis on society. The influx into the heartland dilutes and weakens our local rural communities. We are rapidly losing our inheritance and our identity.

One other gift I would like to possess is the art of the poet. I am often left in amazement by those people who can link words in a certain way. And I'm pleased to say that some Welsh poets have honoured me in verse.

I am deeply indebted to many people, but two, in particular, deserve my undying gratitude. My wife Olwen, and my son John come first, naturally – not forgetting his wife, Niki and our grand-daughter, Celine. John is our only child, and when anyone refers to that fact I tell them, 'Following John's birth I lost the recipe.' And both Olwen and John have been my strength, as have Olwen's family. Her brother has come to the rescue often when I have been called away. Thanks to these I have never had to falter. And the hired hands that have worked for me over the years have been unstinting in their contribution. If it hadn't been for all these it would have been impossible for me to have achieved so much.

But outside my family and helpers I must name two people in particular. For one thing, I have spent a good part of my life in their company. One of them is Geraint Rees, the director of *Cefn Gwlad*. We have worked together for well over 20 years now. And even though we sometimes have our different ways of looking at things they have been very happy years. I am rather impulsive and blunt. He is patient and calm.

The second is Marian Hughes, the P.A., or the production assistant. She is ideally suited to the work involved. She knows the ways of country people. She knows their very thoughts and respects them. She knows how to handle them. And in the media world that is all-important.

Working on *Cefn Gwlad* and the other various television and radio series has been an honour for me. But bestowed honours have also added to the icing on my cake. Through my work I have met people that I would not normally have been able to meet in a month of Sundays. These include Her Majesty the Queen, the late Queen Mother, the Prince of Wales and Princess Anne, or Mrs Phillips, as I once described her. I was made an Associate of the Royal Agricultural Society as a reward for my contribution to country life. I was made Vice-President of the Welsh Black Cattle Society, which meant that I became President during its centenary year. For four years I was President of the Welsh Sheepdog Trials Society. I was presented with a prize by the Farmers' Union of Wales for the best agricultural television documentary. I was awarded a BAFTA award for *Away with Dai* as well as a prize for the best humorous programme for *Dai ar y Piste,* and a *Cefn Gwlad* special also won an award. And to cap it all, when S4C celebrated its 20th birthday, *Cefn Gwlad* was voted Best Programme Ever by viewers in Wales. And in January 2004, BAFTA chose to honour me with the award of a Fellowship for my contribution to the broadcasting industry for 35 years. All these honours belong not to me as an individual, but to all those with whom I have worked.

Probably the greatest honour to come my way was to be presented with the Sir Brynner Jones Memorial Award at the Royal Welsh Show for my contribution to agriculture. I received it at the show that marked the Royal Welsh Society's Centenary Year.

Perhaps the most unlikely tribute paid to me, however, was to have a horse named after me. As part of the series on trotting races, *Rasus*, I visited the world's largest pacers' stud in Harrisburg, Pennsylvania. Pacers, by the way, have a rather different movement to trotters. The Hanover Show Farm, owned by Williams and Gaitskill has 920 breeding mares and is renowned worldwide. Williams's great-great-grandfather was a miner in Porth in the Rhondda. All their horses bear the suffix Hanover. I was delighted when they named one of their yearling colts Dai Jones Hanover. One drawback is that some people insist on calling it Dai Jones's Hangover.

Despite my successes in various fields I have one great ambition left to realize. Yes, I have won the coveted Blue Ribbon at both the National and Llangollen. One of my animals won the Welsh Black section and in doing so received the Queen's Cup at Smithfield. I was chosen, with Mal, my dog, to represent Wales in the International Sheepdogs Trials. But there remains one dream – to win the Welsh Black championship at the Royal Welsh Show with a cow or bull that I have bred myself.

We in Wales have witnessed many changes. But our poets over the years have sung of the ever-turning circle. My only wish now is for the good health that will see me through.

Here is another truth I can state with my hand on my heart. I have accepted invitations to countless concerts and variety shows; I have adjudicated in all kinds of competitions; I have conducted many a *Gymanfa Ganu*; I have chaired all kinds of events from Anglesey to Monmouth, from Aberystwyth to Presteigne. But I have never charged one penny for performing in my own Ceredigion. And I sincerely hope that I can still boast that fact at the end of my career. Had I ever asked for money from my fellow Cardis, the very people that have nurtured me, I would not be able to sleep in my bed at night.

Of all the foreign countries I have had the pleasure of visiting, should I be able to return to spend a fortnight or three weeks there, I would choose Kenya – back to the wild-life on the Masai Mara and the Serengeti. Back to the native tribes that populate those areas. They are exceptional people. They are people who possess a common tribal memory. They have dignity. They are a proud and welcoming people.

I could not close without thanking those who gave me a sense of purpose at the local Young Farmers' Club at Llangwrddon, and later on at Llanilar. I was taught early the secrets of appearing and performing in public. And without that tuition I don't think I would have gone anywhere near as far as I have. I felt humbled to have been invited as guest of honour when Llangwrddon YFC celebrated its silver jubilee.

Olwen and I were also closely involved with Llanilar YFC. For ten years during the 80s and 90s we were club leaders. There were around a hundred members but they were inexperienced and did not perform in public. However, they went on to excel in drama, public speaking and stock judging both individually and as a team. Llanilar were County Rally winners six years running. Today, many of those members have gone on to be prominent in many spheres of public life in local government, as adjudicators and as stock buyers.

Although I am known as Dai Llanilar throughout Wales and beyond, Llangwrddon will forever be written on my heart. And when the last curtain call arrives from above, my wish is that I should be returned to Llangwrddon so that I may rest among some of those great personalities that shaped my life, those that have left their indelible stamp on my character. Among them will be Uncle Morgan. Even now I can hear his voice coaxing me, cajoling me, especially so when I tend to drag my feet.

'Now then, boy. Give it a little bit more. Swing that arm and let your armpit feel the wind.'

Immortal, eternal words.